Contents

H

Classic Fishing Stories

Edited and with an Introduction by

NICK LYONS

LYONS PRESS
Guilford, Connecticut
An imprint of Globe Pequot Press

To buy books in quantity for corporate use
or incentives, call **(800) 962-0973**
or e-mail **premiums@GlobePequot.com.**

Lyons Press is an imprint of Globe Pequot Press.

Project editor: Staci Zacharski
Layout artist: Melissa Evarts

Library of Congress Cataloging-in-Publication Data is available on file.

ISBN 978-1-4930-0617-5

Printed in the United States of America

INTRODUCTION

THE INESCAPABLE TRUTH ABOUT ANY "CLASSIC" WRITING IS that it remains classic only insofar as people want to read it. Fishermen of all kinds go back to the early stories about their sport for the simple reason that they enjoy doing so. There are angling historians who study the evolution of tackle or tying techniques, the origins of the dry fly, the innovative genius of this or that early angler, the importance of split bamboo rods, or who first used the urine-stained underbelly of a vixen to imitate the body of a female *Ephemerella subvaria*. But the great stories about fishing, and the memoirs, recollections, and meditations, are read and re-read only because they give pleasure, because they are entertaining in themselves, and because they tell us something interesting about the mysterious passion for fishing.

Passion. That's the word that links most fishermen and most of the stories in this collection. We are passionate about fishing in a way uncommon for a mere sport; for angling combines so many discrete skills and qualities, from the intimate connection to the natural world that it provides, to its unique friendships, the need for an orchestra of skills, its odd admixture of hope and frustration, the intensity that comes with its peculiar territory. And the passion often enough starts early. The ten-year-old boy in "The River God"—which has long been one of my great favorites—idolizes the great seventy-year-old colonel, his best friend, his river god, and is simply mad about fishing. When his father says, "you can't always fish," he replies that he can, and reflects, "I was right and have proved it for thirty years and more." And when his father asks if it isn't "dull not catching anything," the boy replies honestly, as he says he has done a thousand times since, "As if it could be."

The passion in Viscount Grey of Fallodon's "Retrospect" is of an entirely different stripe—reflective, deepened by years and layers of experience of the most diverse sort, redolent with precious memories, tempered by the intelligence of a wise and worldly man; it is like a fire of banked red coals, giving even more and steadier heat than the blazing fires of youth.

Between these, the first and last stories in this collection, there are a great variety of other manifestations of the fishing passion. There are the quiet pleasures of fishing with a worm in Bliss Perry's thoughtful counterpiece to the complex world of fly fishing; the hilarity of that most chauvinist story of man-fisherman and wife, failing miserably, John Taintor Foote's "A Wedding Gift"; the failure of quite another sort in Henry Van Dyke's wonderful "A Fatal Success," where a man is too successful in inducting his wife into the delights of fishing; high jinx, puckishness, and a happy kind of "in" humor in pieces like Rudyard Kipling's "On Dry-Cow Fishing As A Fine

Art" and other stories; an unforgettable look at it all from the trout's point of view in Roland Pertwee's brilliant "Fish Are Such Liars"; and the dangers, when the reckoning comes after death, of having been quite too much of a fishing nut in G. E. M. Skues's famous "Mr. Theodore Castwell." A large number of literary lights have written about angling and you will find herein some fine stories by R. D. Blackmore, John Buchan, Anton Chekhov, Guy de Maupassant, Andrew Lang, and even Lewis Carroll.

It is a full and diverse collection, I think, including twenty of the best of the older pieces, out of at least a hundred I might have selected. I first read many of them more than forty years ago, and I read them regularly still. All of these pieces have, as the phrase goes, stood the test of a lot of time. I hope readers will find them as enduring, as interesting, as revealing as I do.

Nick Lyons

The River God

Roland Pertwee

WHEN I WAS A LITTLE BOY I HAD A FRIEND WHO WAS A colonel. He was not the kind of colonel you meet nowadays, who manages a motor showroom in the West End of London and wears crocodile shoes and a small mustache and who calls you "old man" and slaps your back, independent of the fact that you may have been no more than a private in the war. My colonel was of the older order that takes a third of a century and a lot of Indian sun and Madras curry in the making. A veteran of the Mutiny he was, and wore side whiskers to prove it. Once he came upon a number of Sepoys conspiring mischief in a byre with a barrel of gunpowder. So he put the butt of his cheroot into the barrel and presently they all went to hell. That was the kind of man he was in the way of business.

In the way of pleasure he was very different. In the way of pleasure he wore an old Norfolk coat that smelt of heather and brine, and which had no elbows to speak of. And he wore a Sherlock Holmesy kind of cap with a swarm of salmon flies upon it, that to my boyish fancy was more splendid than a crown. I cannot remember his legs, because they were nearly always under water, hidden in great canvas waders. But once he sent me a photograph of himself riding on a tricycle, so I expect he had some knickerbockers, too, which would have been that tight kind, with box cloth under the knees. Boys don't take much stock of clothes. His head occupied my imagination. A big, brave, white-haired head with cherry-red rugose cheeks and honest, laughing, puckered eyes, with gunpowder marks in their corners.

People at the little Welsh fishing inn where we met said he was a bore; but I knew him to be a god and shall prove it.

I was ten years old and his best friend.

He was seventy something and my hero.

Properly I should not have mentioned my hero so soon in this narrative. He belongs to a later epoch, but sometimes it is forgivable to start with a boast, and now that I have committed myself I lack the courage to call upon my colonel to fall back two paces to the rear, quick march, and wait until he is wanted.

The real beginning takes place, as I remember, somewhere in Hampshire on the Grayshott Road, among sandy banks, sentinel firs and plum-colored wastes of heather. Summer-holiday time it was, and I was among folks whose names have since vanished like lizards under the stones of forgetfulness. Perhaps it was a picnic walk; perhaps I carried a basket and was told not to swing it for fear of bursting its cargo of ginger beer. In those days ginger beer had big bulgy corks held down with a string. In a hot sun or under stress of too much agitation the string would break and the corks fly. Then there would be a merry foaming fountain and someone would get reproached.

One of our company had a fishing rod. He was a young man who, one day, was to be an uncle of mine. But that didn't concern me. What concerned me was the fishing rod and presently—perhaps because he felt he must keep in with the family—he let me carry it. To the fisherman born there is nothing so provoking of curiosity as a fishing rod in a case.

Surreptitiously I opened the flap, which contained a small grass spear in a wee pocket, and, pulling down the case a little, I admired the beauties of the cork butt, with its gun-metal ferrule and reel rings and the exquisite frail slenderness of the two top joints.

"It's got two top joints—two!" I exclaimed ecstatically.

"Of course," said he. "All good trout rods have two."

I marveled in silence at what seemed to me then a combination of extravagance and excellent precaution.

There must have been something inherently understanding and noble about that young man who would one day be my uncle, for, taking me by the arm, he sat me down on a tuft of heather and took the pieces of rod from the case and fitted them together. The rest of the company moved on and left me in Paradise.

It is thirty-five years ago since that moment and not one detail of it is forgotten. There sounds in my ears today as clearly as then, the faint, clear pop made by the little cork stoppers with their boxwood tops as they were withdrawn. I remember how, before fitting the pieces together, he rubbed the ferrules against the side of his nose to prevent them sticking. I remember looking up the length of it through a tunnel of sneck rings to the eyelet at the end. Not until he had fixed a reel and passed a line through the rings did he put the lovely thing into my hand. So light it was, so firm, so persuasive; such a thing alive—a scepter. I could do no more than say "Oo!" and again, "Oo!"

"A thrill, ain't it?" said he.

I had no need to answer that. In my new-found rapture was only one sorrow—the knowledge that such happiness would not endure and that, all too soon, a blank and rodless future awaited me.

"They must be awfully—awfully 'spensive," I said.

"Couple of guineas," he replied offhandedly.

A couple of guineas! And we were poor folk and the future was more rodless than ever.

"Then I shall save and save and save," I said.

And my imagination started to add up twopence a week into guineas. Two hundred and forty pennies to the pound, multiplied by two—four hundred and eighty—and then another twenty-four pennies—five hundred and four. Why, it would take a lifetime, and no sweets, no elastic for catapults, no penny novelty boxes or air-gun bullets or ices or anything. Tragedy must have been writ large upon my face, for he said suddenly, "When's your birthday?"

I was almost ashamed to tell him how soon it was. Perhaps he, too, was a little taken aback by its proximity, for that future uncle of mine was not so rich as uncles should be.

"We must see about it."

"But it wouldn't—it couldn't be one like that," I said.

I must have touched his pride, for he answered loftily, "Certainly it will."

In the fortnight that followed I walked on air and told everybody I had as good as got a couple-of-guineas rod.

No one can deceive a child, save the child himself, and when my birthday came and with it a long brown paper parcel, I knew, even before I had removed the wrappers, that this two-guinea rod was not worth the money. There was a brown linen case, it is true, but it was not a case with a neat compartment for each joint, nor was there a spear in the flap. There was only one top instead of two, and there were no popping little stoppers to protect the ferrules from dust and injury. The lower joint boasted no elegant cork hand piece, but was a tapered affair coarsely made and rudely varnished. When I fitted the pieces together, what I balanced in my hand was tough and stodgy, rather than limber. The reel, which had come in a different parcel, was of wood. It had neither check nor brake, the line overran and backwound itself with distressing frequency.

I had not read and reread Gamages' price list without knowing something of rods, and I did not need to look long at this rod before realizing that it was no match to the one I had handled on the Grayshott Road.

I believe at first a great sadness possessed me, but very presently imagination came to the rescue. For I told myself that I had only to think that this was the rod of all other rods that I desired most and it would be so. And it was so.

Furthermore, I told myself that, in this great wide ignorant world, but few people existed with such expert knowledge of rods as I possessed. That I had but to say, "here is the final word in good rods," and they would accept it as such.

Very confidently I tried the experiment on my mother, with inevitable success. From the depths of her affection and her ignorance on all such matters, she produced:

"It's a magnificent rod."

I went my way, knowing full well that she knew not what she said, but that she was kind.

With rather less confidence I approached my father, saying, "Look, father! It cost two guineas. It's absolutely the best sort you can get."

And he, after waggling it a few moments in silence, quoted cryptically:

"There is nothing either good or bad but thinking makes it so."

Young as I was, I had some curiosity about words, and on any other occasion I would have called on him to explain. But this I did not do, but left hurriedly, for fear that he should explain.

In the two years that followed I fished every day in the slip of a back garden of our tiny London house. And, having regard to the fact that this rod was never fashioned to throw a fly, I acquired a pretty knack in the fullness of time and performed some glib casting at the nasturtiums and marigolds that flourished by the back wall.

My parents' fortunes must have been in the ascendant, I suppose, for I call to mind an unforgettable breakfast when my mother told me that father had decided we should spend our summer holiday at a Welsh hotel on the river Lledr. The place was called Pont-y-pant, and she showed me a picture of the hotel with a great knock-me-down river creaming past the front of it.

Although in my dreams I had heard fast water often enough, I had never seen it, and the knowledge that in a month's time I should wake with the music of a cataract in my ears was almost more than patience could endure.

In that exquisite, intolerable period of suspense I suffered as only childish longing and enthusiasm can suffer. Even the hank of gut that I bought and bent into innumerable casts failed to alleviate that suffering. I would walk for miles for a moment's delight captured in gluing my nose to the windows of tackleists' shops in the West End. I learned from my grandmother—a wise and calm old lady—how to make nets and, having mastered the art, I made myself a landing net. This I set up on a frame fashioned from a penny schoolmaster's cane bound to an old walking stick. It would be pleasant to record that this was a good and serviceable net, but it was not. It flopped over in a very distressing fashion when called upon to lift the lightest weight. I had to confess to myself that I had more enthusiasm than skill in the manufacture of such articles.

At school there was a boy who had a fishing creel, which he swapped with me for a Swedish knife, a copy of *Rogues of the Fiery Cross*, and an Easter egg which I had kept on account of its rare beauty. He had forced a hard bargain and was sure he had the best of it, but I knew otherwise.

At last the great day dawned, and after infinite travel by train we reached our destination as the glow of sunset was graying into dark. The river was in spate, and as we crossed a tall stone bridge on our way to the hotel I heard it below me, barking and grumbling among great rocks. I was pretty far gone in tiredness, for I remember little else that night but a rod rack in the hall—a dozen rods of different sorts and sizes, with gaudy salmon flies, some nets, a gaff and an oak coffer upon which lay a freshly caught salmon on a blue ashet. Then supper by candlelight, bed, a glitter of stars through the open window, and the ceaseless drumming of water.

By six o'clock next morning I was on the river bank, fitting my rod together and watching in awe the great brown ribbon of water go fleetly by.

Among my most treasured possessions were half a dozen flies, and two of these I attached to the cast with exquisite care. While so engaged, a shadow fell on the grass beside me and, looking up, I beheld a lank, shabby individual with a walrus mustache and an unhealthy face who, the night before, had helped with our luggage at the station.

"Water's too heavy for flies," said he, with an uptilting inflection. "This evening, yes; now, no—none whateffer. Better try with a worrum in the burrun."

He pointed at a busy little brook which tumbled down the steep hillside and joined the main stream at the garden end.

"C-couldn't I fish with a fly in the—the burrun?" I asked, for although I wanted to catch a fish very badly, for honor's sake I would fain take it on a fly.

"Indeed, no," he replied, slanting the tone of his voice skyward. "You cootn't. Neffer. And that isn't a fly rod whateffer."

"It is," I replied hotly. "Yes, it is."

But he only shook his head and repeated, "No," and took the rod from my hand and illustrated its awkwardness and handed it back with a wretched laugh.

If he had pitched me into the river I should have been happier.

"It is a fly rod and it cost two guineas," I said, and my lower lip trembled.

"Neffer," he repeated. "Five shillings would be too much."

Even a small boy is entitled to some dignity.

Picking up my basket, I turned without another word and made for the hotel. Perhaps my eyes were blinded with tears, for I was about to plunge into the dark hall when a great, rough, kindly voice arrested me with:

"Easy does it."

At the thick end of an immense salmon rod there strode out into the sunlight the noblest figure I had ever seen.

There is no real need to describe my colonel again—I have done so already—but the temptation is too great. Standing in the doorway, the sixteen-foot rod in hand, the deer-stalker hat, besprent with flies, crowning his shaggy head, the waders, like seven-league boots, braced up to his armpits, the creel across his shoulder, a gaff across his back, he looked what he was—a god. His eyes met mine with that kind of smile one good man keeps for another.

"An early start," he said. "Any luck, old fellar?"

I told him I hadn't started—not yet.

"Wise chap," said he. "Water's a bit heavy for trouting. It'll soon run down, though. Let's vet those flies of yours."

He took my rod and whipped it expertly.

"A nice piece—new, eh?"

"N-not quite," I stammered; "but I haven't used it yet, sir, in water."

That god read men's minds.

"I know—garden practice; capital; nothing like it."

Releasing my cast, he frowned critically over the flies—a Blue Dun and a March Brown.

"Think so?" he queried. "You don't think it's a shade late in the season for these fancies?" I said I thought perhaps it was. "Yes, I think you're right," said he. "I believe in this big water you'd do better with a livelier pattern. Teal and Red, Cock-y-bundy, Greenwell's Glory."

I said nothing, but nodded gravely at these brave names.

Once more he read my thoughts and saw through the

wicker sides of my creel a great emptiness.

"I expect you've fished most in southern rivers. These Welsh trout have a fancy for a spot of color."

He rummaged in the pocket of his Norfolk jacket and produced a round tin which once had held saddle soap.

"Collar on to that," said he; "there's a proper pickle of flies and casts in that tin that, as a keen fisherman, you won't mind sorting out. Still, they may come in useful."

"But, I say, you don't mean—" I began.

"Yes, go in; stick to it. All fishermen are members of the same club and I'm giving the trout a rest for a bit." His eyes ranged the hills and trees opposite. "I must be getting on with it before the sun's too high."

Waving his free hand, he strode away and presently was lost to view at a bend in the road.

I think my mother was a little piqued by my abstraction during breakfast. My eyes never, for an instant, deserted the round tin box which lay open beside my plate. Within it were a paradise and a hundred miracles all tangled together in the pleasantest disorder. My mother said something about a lovely walk over the hills, but I had other plans, which included a very glorious hour which should be spent untangling and wrapping up in neat squares of paper my new treasures.

"I suppose he knows best what he wants to do," she said.

So it came about that I was left alone and betook myself to a sheltered spot behind a rock where all the delicious disorder was remedied and I could take stock of what was mine.

I am sure there were at least six casts all set up with flies, and ever so many loose flies and one great stout, tapered cast, with a salmon fly upon it, that was so rich in splendor that I doubted if my benefactor could really have known that it was there.

I felt almost guilty at owning so much, and not until I had done full justice to everything did I fasten a new cast to my line and go a-fishing.

There is a lot said and written about beginners' luck, but none of it came my way. Indeed, I spent most of the morning extricating my line from the most fearsome tangles. I had no skill in throwing a cast with two droppers upon it and I found it was an art not to be learned in a minute. Then, from overeagerness, I was too snappy with my back cast, whereby, before many minutes had gone, I heard that warning crack behind me that betokens the loss of a tail fly. I must have spent half an hour searching the meadow for that lost fly and finding it not. Which is not strange, for I wonder has any fisherman ever found that lost fly. The reeds, the buttercups, and the little people with many legs who run in the wet grass conspire together to keep the secret of its hiding place. I gave up at last, and with a feeling of shame that was only proper, I invested a new fly on the point of my cast and set to work again, but more warily.

In that hard racing water a good strain was put upon my rod, and before the morning was out it was creaking at the joints in a way that kept my heart continually in my mouth. It is the duty of a rod to work with a single smooth action and by no means to divide its performance into three sections of activity. It is a hard task for any angler to persuade his line austerely if his rod behaves thus.

When, at last, my father strolled up the river bank, walking, to his shame, much nearer the water than a good fisherman should, my nerves were jumpy from apprehension.

"Come along. Food's ready. Done any good?" said he.

Again it was to his discredit that he put food before sport, but I told him I had had a wonderful morning, and he was glad.

"What do you want to do this afternoon, old man?" he asked.

"Fish," I said.

"But you can't always fish," he said.

I told him I could, and I was right and have proved it for thirty years and more.

"Well, well," he said, "please yourself, but isn't it dull not catching anything?"

And I said, as I've said a thousand times since, "As if it could be."

So that afternoon I went downstream instead of up, and found myself in difficult country where the river boiled between the narrows of two hills. Stunted oaks overhung the water and great boulders opposed its flow. Presently I came to a sort of natural flight of steps—a pool and a cascade three times repeated—and there, watching the maniac fury of the waters in awe and wonderment, I saw the most stirring sight in my young life. I saw a silver salmon leap superbly from the caldron below into the pool above. And I saw another and another salmon do likewise. And I wonder the eyes of me did not fall out of my head.

I cannot say how long I stayed watching that gallant pageant of leaping fish—in ecstasy there is no measurement of time—but at last it came upon me that all the salmon in the sea were careering past me and that if I were to realize my soul's desire I must hasten to the pool below before the last of them had gone by.

It was a mad adventure, for until I had discovered that stout cast, with the gaudy fly attached in the tin box, I had given no thought to such noble quarry. My recent possessions had put ideas into my head above my station and beyond my powers. Failure, however, means little to the young and, walking fast, yet gingerly, for fear of breaking my rod top against a tree, I followed the path downstream until I came to a great basin of water into which, through a narrow throat the river thundered like a storm.

At the head of the pool was a plate of rock scored by the nails of fishermen's boots, and here I sat me down to wait while the salmon cast, removed from its wrapper, was allowed to soak and soften in a puddle left by the rain.

And while I waited a salmon rolled not ten yards from where I sat. Head and tail, up and down he went, a great monster of a fish, sporting and deriding me.

With that performance so near at hand, I have often wondered how I was able to control my fingers well enough to tie a figure-eight knot between the line and the cast. But I did, and I'm proud to be able to record it. Your true-born angler does not go blindly to work until he has first satisfied his conscience. There is a pride, in knots, of which the laity knows nothing, and if, through neglect to tie them rightly, failure and loss should result, pride may not be restored nor conscience salved by the plea of eagerness. With my trembling fingers I bent the knot and, with a pummeling heart, launched the line into the broken water at the throat of the pool.

At first the mere tug of the water against that large fly was so thrilling to me that it was hard to believe that I had not hooked a whale. The trembling line swung round in a wide arc into a calm eddy below where I stood. Before casting afresh I shot a glance over my shoulder to assure myself there was no limb of a tree behind me to foul the fly. And this was a gallant cast, true and straight, with a couple of yards more length than its predecessor, and a wider radius. Instinctively I knew, as if the surface had been marked with an X where the salmon had risen, that my fly must pass right over the spot. As it swung by, my nerves were strained like piano wires. I think I knew something tremendous, impossible, terrifying, was going to happen. The sense, the certitude was so strong in me that I half opened my mouth to shout a warning to the monster, not to.

I must have felt very, very young in that moment. I, who that same day had been talked to as a man by a man among men. The years were stripped from me and I was what I was—ten years old and appalled. And then, with the suddenness of a rocket, it happened. The water was cut into a swath. I remember a silver loop bearing downward—a bright, shining, vanishing thing like the bobbin of my mother's sewing machine—and a tug. I shall never forget the viciousness of that tug. I had my fingers tight upon the line, so I got the full force of it. To counteract a tendency to go headfirst into the spinning water below, I threw myself backward and sat down on the hard rock with a jar that shut my teeth on my tongue—like the jaws of a trap.

Luckily I had let the rod go out straight with the line, else it must have snapped in the first frenzy of the downstream rush. Little ass that I was, I tried to check the speeding line with my forefinger, with the result that it cut and burnt me to the bone. There wasn't above twenty yards of line in the reel, and the wretched contrivance was trying to be rid of the line even faster than the fish was wrenching it out. Heaven knows why it didn't snarl, for great loops and whorls were whirling, like Catherine wheels, under my wrist. An instant's glance revealed the terrifying fact that there was not more than half a dozen yards left on the reel and the fish showed no sign of abating his rush. With the realization of impending and inevitable catastrophe upon me, I launched a yell for help, which, rising above the roar of the waters, went echoing down the gorge.

And then, to add to my terrors, the salmon leaped—a winging leap like a silver arch appearing and instantly disappearing upon the broken surface. So mighty, so all-powerful he seemed in that sublime moment that I lost all sense of reason and raised the rod, with a sudden jerk, above my head.

I have often wondered, had the rod actually been the two-guinea rod my imagination claimed for it, whether it could have withstood the strain thus violently and unreasonably imposed upon it. The wretched thing that I held so grimly never even put up a fight. It snapped at the ferrule of the lower joint and plunged like a toboggan down the slanting line, to vanish into the black depths of the water.

My horror at this calamity was so profound that I was lost even to the consciousness that the last of my line had run out. A couple of vicious tugs advised me of this awful truth. Then, snap! The line parted at the reel, flickered out through the rings and was gone. I was left with nothing but the butt of a broken rod in my hand and an agony of mind that even now I cannot recall without emotion.

I am not ashamed to confess that I cried. I lay down on the rock, with my cheek in the puddle where I had soaked the cast, and plenished it with my tears. For what had the future left for me but a cut and burning finger, a badly bumped behind, the single joint of a broken rod and no faith in uncles? How long I lay there weeping I do not know. Ages, perhaps, or minutes, or seconds.

I was roused by a rough hand on my shoulder and a kindly voice demanding, "Hurt yourself, Ike Walton?"

Blinking away my tears, I pointed at my broken rod with a bleeding forefinger.

"Come! This is bad luck," said my colonel, his face grave as a stone. "How did it happen?"

"I c-caught a s-salmon."

"You what?" said he.

"I d-did," I said.

He looked at me long and earnestly; then, taking my injured hand, he looked at that and nodded.

"The poor groundlings who can find no better use for a river than something to put a bridge over think all fishermen are liars," said he. "But we know better, eh? By the bumps and breaks and cuts I'd say you made a plucky fight against heavy odds. Let's hear all about it."

So, with his arm round my shoulders and his great shaggy head near to mine, I told him all about it.

At the end he gave me a mighty and comforting squeeze, and he said, "The loss of one's first big fish is the heaviest loss I know. One feels, whatever happens, one'll never—" He stopped and pointed dramatically. "There is goes—see! Down there at the tail of the pool!"

In the broken water where the pool emptied itself into the shallows beyond, I saw the top joints of my rod dancing on the surface.

"Come on!" he shouted, and gripping my hand, jerked me to my feet. "Scatter your legs! There's just a chance!"

Dragging me after him, we raced along by the river path to the end of the pool, where, on a narrow promontory of grass, his enormous salmon rod was lying.

"Now," he said, picking it up and making the line whistle to and fro in the air with sublime authority, "keep your eyes skinned on those shallows for another glimpse of it."

A second later I was shouting, "There! There!"

He must have seen the rod point at the same moment, for

his line flowed out and the big fly hit the water with a plop not a couple of feet from the spot.

He let it ride on the current, playing it with a sensitive touch like the brushwork of an artist.

"Half a jiffy!" he exclaimed at last. "Wait! Yes, I think so. Cut down to that rock and see if I haven't fished up the line."

I needed no second invitation, and presently was yelling, "Yes—yes, you have!"

"Stretch yourself out then and collar hold of it."

With the most exquisite care he navigated the line to where I lay stretched upon the rock. Then:

"Right you are! Good lad! I'm coming down."

Considering his age, he leaped the rocks like a chamois.

"Now," he said, and took the wet line delicately between his forefinger and thumb. One end trailed limply downstream, but the other end seemed anchored in the big pool where I had my unequal and disastrous contest.

Looking into his face, I saw a sudden light of excitement dancing in his eyes.

"Odd," he muttered, "but not impossible."

"What isn't?" I asked breathlessly.

"Well, it looks to me as if the joints of that rod of yours have gone downstream."

Gingerly he pulled up the line, and presently an end with a broken knot appeared.

"The reel knot, eh?" I nodded gloomily. "Then we lose the rod," said he. That wasn't very heartening news. "On the other hand, it's just possible the fish is still on—sulking."

"Oo!" I exclaimed.

"Now, steady does it," he warned, "and give me my rod."

Taking a pair of clippers from his pocket, he cut his own line just above the cast.

"Can you tie a knot?" he asked.

"Yes," I nodded.

"Come on, then; bend your line onto mine. Quick as lightning."

Under his critical eye, I joined the two lines with a blood knot. "I guessed you were a fisherman," he said, nodded approvingly and clipped off the ends. "And now to know the best or the worst."

I shall never forget the music of that check reel or the suspense with which I watched as, with the butt of the rod bearing against the hollow of his thigh, he steadily wound up the wet slack line. Every instant I expected it to come drifting downstream, but it didn't. Presently it rose in a tight slant from the pool above.

"Snagged, I'm afraid," he said, and worked the rod with an easy straining motion to and fro. "Yes, I'm afraid—no, by Lord Bobs, he's on!"

I think it was only right and proper that I should have launched a yell of triumph as, with the spoken word, the point at which the line cut the water shifted magically from the left side of the pool to the right.

"And a fish too," said he.

In the fifteen minutes that followed, I must have experienced every known form of terror and delight.

"Youngster," said he, "you should be doing this, by rights, but I'm afraid the rod's a bit above your weight."

"Oh, go on and catch him," I pleaded.

"And so I will," he promised; "unship the gaff, young un, and stand by to use it, and if you break the cast we'll never speak to each other again, and that's a bet."

But I didn't break the cast. The noble, courageous, indomitable example of my river god had lent me skill and precision beyond my years. When at long last a weary, beaten, silver monster rolled within reach of my arm into a shallow eddy, the steel gaff shot out fair and true, and sank home.

And then I was lying on the grass, with my arms round a salmon that weighed twenty-two pounds on the scale and contained every sort of happiness known to a boy.

And best of all, my river god shook hands with me and called me "partner."

That evening the salmon was placed upon the blue ashet in the hall, bearing a little card with its weight and my name upon it.

And I am afraid I sat on a chair facing it, for ever so long, so that I could hear what the other anglers had to say as they passed by. I was sitting there when my colonel put his head out of his private sitting room and beckoned me to come in.

"A true fisherman lives in the future, not the past, old man," said he; "though, for this once, it 'ud be a shame to reproach you."

I suppose I colored guilty—at any rate, I hope so.

"We got the fish," said he, "but we lost the rod, and a future without a rod doesn't bear thinking of. Now"—and he pointed at a long wooden box on the floor, that overflowed with rods of different sorts and sizes—"rummage among those. Take your time and see if you can find anything to suit you."

"But do you mean—can I—"

"We're partners, aren't we? And p'r'aps as such you'd rather we went through our stock together."

"Oo, sir," I said.

"Here, quit that," he ordered gruffly. "By Lord Bobs, if a show like this afternoon's don't deserve a medal, what does? Now, here's a handy piece by Hardy—a light and useful tool— or if you fancy greenheart in preference to split bamboo—"

I have the rod to this day, and I count it among my dearest treasures. And to this day I have a flick of the wrist that was his legacy. I have, too, some small skill in dressing flies, the elements of which were learned in his company by candlelight after the day's work was over. And I have countless memories of that month-long, month-short friendship—the closest and most perfect friendship, perhaps, of all my life.

He came to the station and saw me off. How vividly I remember his shaggy head at the window, with the whiskered cheeks and the gunpowder marks at the corners of his eyes! I didn't cry, although I wanted to awfully. We were partners and shook hands. I never saw him again, although on my birthdays I would have colored cards from him, with Irish, Scotch,

Norwegian postmarks. Very brief they were: "Water very low." "Took a good fish last Thursday." "Been prawning, but don't like it."

Sometimes at Christmas I had gifts—a reel, a tapered line, a fly book. But I never saw him again.

Came at last no more cards or gifts, but in the *Fishing Gazette*, of which I was a religious reader, was an obituary telling how one of the last of the Mutiny veterans had joined the great majority. It seems he had been fishing half an hour before he died. He had taken his rod down and passed out. They had buried him at Totnes, overlooking the River Dart.

So he was no more—my river god—and what was left of him they had put into a box and buried it in the earth.

But that isn't true; nor is it true that I never saw him again. For I seldom go a-fishing but that I meet him on the river banks.

The banks of a river are frequented by a strange company and are full of mysterious and murmurous sounds—the cluck and laughter of water, the piping of birds, the hum of insects, and the whispering of wind in the willows. What should prevent a man in such a place having a word and speech with another who is not there? So much of fishing lies in imagination, and mine needs little stretching to give my river god a living form.

"With this ripple," says he, "you should do well."

"And what's it to be," say I—"Blue Upright, Red Spinner? What's your fancy, sir?"

Spirits never grow old. He has begun to take an interest in dry-fly methods—that river god of mine, with his seven-league boots, his shaggy head, and the gaff across his back.

Crocker's Hole

R. D. Blackmore

I

THE CULM, WHICH RISES IN SOMERSETSHIRE, AND HASTENING into a fairer land (as the border waters wisely do) falls into the Exe near Killerton, formerly was a lovely trout stream, such as perverts the Devonshire angler from due respect toward Father Thames and the other canals round London. In the Devonshire valleys it is sweet to see how soon a spring becomes a rill, and a rill runs on into a rivulet and a rivulet swells into a brook; and before one has time to say, "What are you at?"—before the first tree it ever spoke to is a dummy, or the first hill it ever ran down has turned blue, here we have all the airs and graces, demands and assertions of a full-grown river.

But what is the test of a river? Who shall say? "The power to drown a man," replies the river darkly. But rudeness is not argument. Rather shall we say that the power to work a good undershot wheel, without being dammed up all night in a pond, and leaving a tidy back stream to spare at the bottom of the orchard, is a fair certificate of riverhood. If so, many

Devonshire streams attain that rank within five miles of their spring; aye, and rapidly add to it. At every turn they gather aid, from ash-clad dingle and aldered meadow, mossy rock and ferny wall, hedge-trough-roofed with bramble netting, where the baby water lurks, and lanes that coming down to ford bring suicidal tribute. Arrogant, all-engrossing river, now it has claimed a great valley of its own; and whatever falls within the hill scoop sooner or later belongs to itself. Even the crystal "shutt" that crosses the farmyard by the woodrick, and glides down an aqueduct of last year's bark for Mary to fill the kettle from; and even the tricklets that have no organs for telling or knowing their business, but only get into unwary oozings in and among the water grass, and there make moss and forget themselves among it—one and all, they come to the same thing at last, and that is the river.

The Culm used to be a good river at Culmstock, tormented already by a factory, but not strangled as yet by a railroad. How is it now the present writer does not know, and is afraid to ask, having heard of a vile "Culm Valley Line." But Culmstock bridge was a very pretty place to stand and contemplate the ways of trout; which is easier work than to catch them. When I was just big enough to peep above the rim, or to lie upon it with one leg inside for fear of tumbling over, what a mighty river it used to seem, for it takes a treat there and spreads itself. Above the bridge the factory stream falls in again, having done its business, and washing its hands in the innocent half that has strayed down the meadows. Then under the arches they both rejoice and come to a slide of about two feet, and make a short, wide pool below, and indulge themselves in perhaps two islands, through which a little river always magnifies itself and maintains a mysterious middle. But after that, all of it used to come together, and make off in one body for the meadows, intent upon nurturing trout with rapid stickles, and butter-cuppy corners where fat flies may tumble in. And here you may find in the very first meadow, or at any rate you might have found, forty years ago, the celebrated "Crocker's Hole."

The story of Crocker is unknown to me, and interesting as it doubtless was, I do not deal with him, but with his Hole. Tradition said that he was a baker's boy who, during his basket rounds, fell in love with a maiden who received the cottage loaf, or perhaps good "Households," for her master's use. No doubt she was charming, as a girl should be, but whether she encouraged the youthful baker and then betrayed him with false role, or whether she "consisted" throughout—as our cousins across the water express it—is known to their *manes* only. Enough that she would not have the floury lad; and that he, after giving in his books and money, sought an untimely grave among the trout. And this was the first pool below the bread walk deep enough to drown a five-foot baker boy. Sad it was; but such things must be, and bread must still be delivered daily.

A truce to such reflections—as our foremost writers always say, when they do not see how to go on with them—but it is a serious thing to know what Crocker's Hole was like; because at a time when (if he had only persevered, and married the maid, and succeeded to the oven, and reared a large family of short-weight bakers) he might have been leaning on his crutch beside the pool, and teaching his grandson to swim by precept (that beautiful proxy for practice)—at such a time, I say, there lived a remarkable fine trout in that hole. Anglers are notoriously truthful, especially as to what they catch, or even more frequently have not caught. Though I may have written fiction, among many other sins—as a nice old lady told me once— now I have to deal with facts; and foul scorn would I count it ever to make believe that I caught that fish. My length at that time was not more than the butt of a four-jointed rod, and all I could catch was a minnow with a pin, which our cook Lydia would not cook, but used to say, "Oh, what a shame, Master Richard! They would have been trout in the summer, please God! if you would only a' let 'em grow on." She is living now and will bear me out in this.

But upon every great occasion there arises a great man; or to put it more accurately, in the present instance, a mighty and distinguished boy. My father, being the parson of the parish, and getting, need it be said, small pay, took sundry pupils, very pleasant fellows, about to adorn the universities. Among them was the original "Bude Light," as he was satirically called at Cambridge, for he came from Bude, and there was no light in him. Among them also was John Pike, a born Zebedee if ever there was one.

John Pike was a thickset younker, with a large and bushy head, keen blue eyes that could see through water, and the proper slouch of shoulder into which great anglers ripen; but greater still are born with it; and of these was Master John. It mattered little what the weather was, and scarcely more as to the time of year, John Pike must have his fishing every day, and on Sundays he read about it, and made flies. All the rest of the time he was thinking about it.

My father was coaching him in the fourth book of *The Aeneid* and all those wonderful species of Dido, where passion disdains construction; but the only line Pike cared for was of horsehair. "I fear, Mr. Pike, that you are not giving me your entire attention," my father used to say in his mild dry way; and once when Pike was more than usually abroad, his tutor begged to share his meditations. "Well, sir," said Pike, who was very truthful, "I can see a green drake by the strawberry tree, the first of the season, and your derivation of 'barbarous' put me in mind of my barberry dye." In those days it was a very nice point to get the right tint for the mallard's feather.

No sooner was lesson done than Pike, whose rod was ready upon the lawn, dashed away always for the river, rushing head-long down the hill, and away to the left through a private yard, where "No Thoroughfare" was put up and a big dog stationed to enforce it. But Cerberus himself could not have stopped John Pike; his conscience backed him up in trespass the most sinful when his heart was inditing of a trout upon the rise.

All this, however, is preliminary, as the boy said when he put his father's coat upon his grandfather's tenterhooks, with felonious intent upon his grandmother's apples; the main point to be understood in this, that nothing—neither brazen tower, hundred-eyed Argus, nor Cretan Minotaur—could stop John Pike from getting at a good stickle. But, even as the world knows nothing of its greatest men, its greatest men know nothing of the world beneath their very nose, till fortune sneezes dexter. For two years John Pike must have been whipping the water as hard as Xerxes, without having ever once dreamed of the glorious trout that lived in Crocker's Hole. But why, when he ought to have been at least on bowing terms with every fish as long as his middle finger, why had he failed to know this champion? The answer is simple—because of his short cuts. Flying as he did like an arrow from a bow, Pike used to hit his beloved river at an elbow, some furlong below Crocker's Hole, where a sweet little stickle sailed away downstream, whereas for the length of a meadow upward the water lay smooth, clear, and shallow; therefore the youth, with so little time to spare, rushed into the downward joy.

And here it may be noted that the leading maxim of the present period, that man can discharge his duty only by going counter to the stream, was scarcely mooted in those days. My grandfather (who was a wonderful man, if he was accustomed to fill a cart in two days of fly fishing on the Barle) regularly fished downstream; and what more than a cartload need anyone put into his basket?

And surely it is more genial and pleasant to behold our friend the river growing and thriving as we go on, strengthening its voice and enlarging its bosom, and sparkling through each successive meadow with richer plenitude of silver, than to trace it against its own grain and good will toward weakness, and littleness, and immature conceptions.

However, you will say that if John Pike had fished upstream, he would have found this trout much sooner. And that is true; but still, as it was, the trout had more time to grow into such a prize. And the way in which John found him out was this. For some days he had been tormented with a very painful tooth, which even poisoned all the joys of fishing. Therefore he resolved to have it out and sturdily entered the shop of John Sweetland, the village blacksmith, and there paid his sixpence. Sweetland extracted the teeth of the village, whenever they required it, in the simplest and most effectual way. A piece of fine wire was fastened round the tooth, and the other end round the anvil's nose, then the sturdy blacksmith shut the lower half of his shop door, which was about breast-high, with the patient outside and the anvil within; a strong push of the foot upset the anvil, and the tooth flew out like a well-thrown fly.

When John Pike had suffered this very bravely, "Ah, Master Pike," said the blacksmith, with a grin, "I reckon you won't pull out thic there big vish"—the smithy commanded a view of the river—"clever as you be, quite so peart as thiccy."

"What big fish?" asked the boy, with deepest interest, though his mouth was bleeding fearfully.

"Why, that girt mortial of a vish as hath his hover in Crocker's Hole. Zum on 'em saith as a' must be a zammon."

Off went Pike with his handkerchief to his mouth, and after him ran Alec Bolt, one of his fellow pupils, who had come to the shop to enjoy the extraction.

"Oh, my!" was all that Pike could utter, when by craftily posting himself he had obtained a good view of this grand fish.

"I'll lay you a crown you don't catch him!" cried Bolt, an impatient youth, who scorned angling.

"How long will you give me?" asked the wary Pike, who never made rash wagers.

"Oh! till the holidays if you like; or, if that won't do, till Michaelmas."

Now the midsummer holidays were six weeks off—boys used not to talk of "vacations" then, still less of "recesses."

"I think I'll bet you," said Pike, in his slow way, bending forward carefully, with his keen eyes on this monster; "but it would not be fair to take till Michaelmas. I'll bet you a crown that I catch him before the holidays—at least, unless some other fellow does."

II

The day of that most momentous interview must have been the 14th day of May. Of the year I will not be so sure; for children take more note of days than of years, for which the latter have their full revenge thereafter. It must have been the 14th, because the morrow was our holiday, given upon the 15th of May, in honor of a birthday.

Now, John Pike was beyond his years wary as well as

enterprising, calm as well as ardent, quite as rich in patience as in promptitude and vigor. But Alec Bolt was a headlong youth, volatile, hot, and hasty, fit only to fish the Maelstrom, or a torrent of new lava. And the moment he had laid that wager he expected his crown piece; though time, as the lawyers phrase it, was "expressly of the essence of the contract." And now he demanded that Pike should spend the holiday in trying to catch that trout.

"I shall not go near him," that lad replied, "until I have got a new collar." No piece of personal adornment was it, without which he would not act, but rather that which now is called the fly cast, or the gut cast, or the trace, or what it may be. "And another thing," continued Pike; "the bet is off if you go near him, either now or at any other time, without asking my leave first, and then only going as I tell you."

"What do I want with the great slimy beggar?" the arrogant Bolt made answer. "A good rat is worth fifty of him. No fear of my going near him, Pike. You shan't get out of it that way."

Pike showed his remarkable qualities that day, by fishing exactly as he would have fished without having heard of the great Crockerite. He was upon and away upon the millstream before breakfast; and the forenoon he devoted to his favorite course—first down the Craddock stream, a very pretty confluent of the Culm, and from its junction, down the pleasant hams, where the river winds toward Uffculme. It was my privilege to accompany this hero, as his humble Sancho; while Bolt and the faster race went up the river ratting. We were back in time to have Pike's trout (which ranged between two ounces and one half pound) fried for the early dinner; and here it may be lawful to remark that the trout of the Culm are of the very purest excellence, by reason of the flinty bottom, at any rate in these the upper regions. For the valley is the western outlet of the Black Down range, with the Beacon hill upon the north, and the Hackpen long ridge to the south; and beyond that again the Whetstone hill, upon whose western end wark portholes scarped with white grit mark the pits. But flint is the staple of the broad Culm Valley, under good, well-pastured loam; and here are chalcedonies and agate stones.

At dinner everybody had a brace of trout—large for the larger folk, little for the little ones, with coughing and some patting on the back for bones. What of equal purport could the fierce rat hunter show? Pike explained many points in the history of each fish, seeming to know them none the worse, and love them all the better, for being fried. We banqueted, neither a whit did soul get stinted of banquet impartial. Then the wielder of the magic rod very modestly sought leave of absence at the teatime.

"Fishing again, Mr. Pike, I suppose," my father answered pleasantly; "I used to be fond of it at your age; but never so entirely wrapped up in it as you are."

"No, sir; I am not going fishing again. I want to walk to Wellington, to get some things at Cherry's."

"Books, Mr. Pike? Ah! I am very glad of that. But I fear it can only be fly books."

"I want a little Horace for eighteenpence—the Cambridge one just published, to carry in my pocket—and a new hank of gut."

"Which of the two is more important? Put that into Latin, and answer it."

"Utrum pluris facio? Flaccum flocci. Viscera magni." With this vast effort Pike turned as red as any trout spot.

"After that who could refuse you?" said my father. "You always tell the truth, my boy, in Latin or in English."

Although it was a long walk, some fourteen miles to Wellington and back, I got permission to go with Pike; and as we crossed the bridge and saw the tree that overhung Crocker's Hole, I begged him to show me that mighty fish.

"Not a bit of it," he replied. "It would bring the blackguards. If the blackguards once find him out, it is all over with him."

"The blackguards are all in factory now, and I am sure they cannot see us from the windows. They won't be out till five o'clock."

With the true liberality of young England, which abides even now as large and glorious as ever, we always called the free and enlightened operatives of the period by the courteous name above set down, and it must be acknowledged that some of them deserved it, although perhaps they poached with less of science than their sons. But the cowardly murder of fish by liming the water was already prevalent.

Yielding to my request and perhaps his own desire—manfully kept in check that morning—Pike very carefully approached that pool, commanding me to sit down while he reconnoitered from the meadow upon the right bank of the stream. And the place which had so sadly quenched the fire of the poor baker's love filled my childish heart with dread and deep wonder at the cruelty of women. But as for John Pike, all he thought of was the fish and the best way to get at him.

Very likely that hole is "holed out" now, as the Yankees well express it, or at any rate changed out of knowledge. Even in my time a very heavy flood entirely altered its character; but to the eager eye of Pike it seemed pretty much as follows, and possibly it may have come to such a form again:

The river, after passing through a hurdle fence at the head of the meadow, takes a little turn or two of bright and shallow indifference, then gathers itself into a good strong slide, as if going down a slope instead of steps. The right bank is high and beetles over with yellow loam and grassy fringe; but the other side is of flinty shingle, low and bare and washed by floods. At the end of this rapid, the stream turns sharply under an ancient alder tree into a large, deep, calm repose, cool, unruffled, and sheltered from the sun by branch and leaf—and that is the hole of poor Crocker.

At the head of the pool (where the hasty current rushes in so eagerly, with noisy excitement and much ado) the quieter waters from below, having rested and enlarged themselves, come lapping up round either curve, with some recollection of their past career, the hoary experience of foam. And sidling

36

toward the new arrival of the impulsive column, where they meet it, things go on which no man can describe without his mouth being full of water. A V is formed, a fancy letter V, beyond any designer's tracery, and even beyond his imagination, a perpetually fluctuating limpid wedge, perpetually creneled and rippled into by little ups and downs that try to make an impress but can only glide away upon either side or sink in dimples under it. And here a gray bough of the ancient alder stretches across, like a thirsty giant's arm, and makes it a very ticklish place to throw a fly. Yet this was the very spot our John Pike must put his fly into, or lose his crown.

Because the great tenant of Crocker's Hole, who allowed no other fish to wag a fin there, and from strict monopoly had grown so fat, kept his victualing yard—if so low an expression can be used concerning him—without above a square yard of this spot. He had a sweet hover, both for rest and recreation, under the bank, in a placid antre, where the water made no noise, but tickled his belly in digestive ease. The loftier the character is of any being, the slower and more dignified his movements are. No true psychologist could have believed—as Sweetland the blacksmith did, and Mr. Pook the tinman—that this trout could ever be the embodiment of Crocker. For this was the last trout in the universal world to drown himself for love; if truly any trout has done so.

"You may come now, and try to look along my back," John Pike, with a reverential whisper, said to me. "Now, don't be in a hurry, young stupid; kneel down. He is not to be disturbed at his dinner, mind. You keep behind me, and look along my back; I never clapped eyes on such a whopper."

I had to kneel down in a tender reminiscence of pastureland and gaze carefully; and not having eyes like those of our Zebedee (who offered his spine for a camera, as he crawled on all fours in front of me), it took me a long time to descry an object most distinct to all who have that special gift of piercing with their eyes the water. See what is said upon this subject in that delicious book, *The Gamekeeper at Home.*

"You are no better than a muff," said Pike, and it was not in my power to deny it.

"If the sun would only leave off," I said. But the sun, who was having a very pleasant play with the sparkle of the water and the twinkle of the leaves, had no inclination to leave off yet, but kept the rippling crystal in a dance of flashing facets, and the quivering verdure in a steady flush of gold.

But suddenly a May fly, a luscious gray drake, richer and more delicate than canvasback or woodcock, with a dart and a leap and a merry zigzag, began to enjoy a little game above the stream. Rising and falling like a gnat, thrilling her gauzy wings, and arching her elegant pellucid frame, every now and then she almost dipped her three long tapering whisks into the dimples of the water.

"He sees her! He'll have her as sure as a gun!" cried Pike, with a gulp, as if he himself were "rising." "Now can you see him, stupid?"

"Crikey, crokums!" I exclaimed, with classic elegance; "I have seen that long thing for five minutes; but I took it for a tree."

"You little"—animal quite early in the alphabet—"now don't you stir a peg, or I'll dig my elbow into you."

The great trout was stationary almost as a stone, in the middle of the V above described. He was gently fanning with his large clear fins, but holding his own against the current mainly by the wagging of his broad-fluked tail. As soon as my slow eyes had once defined him, he grew upon them mightily, molding himself in the matrix of the water, as a thing put into jelly does. And I doubt whether even John Pike saw him more accurately than I did. His size was such, or seemed to be such, that I fear to say a word about it; not because language does not contain the word, but from dread of exaggeration. But his shape and color may be reasonably told without wounding the feeling of an age whose incredulity springs from self-knowledge.

His head was truly small, his shoulders vast; the spring of his back was like a rainbow when the sun is southing; the generous sweep of his deep elastic belly, nobly pulped out with rich nurture, showed what the power of his brain must be, and seemed to undulate, time for time, with the vibrant vigilance of his large wise eyes. His latter end was consistent also. An elegant taper run of counter, coming almost to a cylinder, as a mackerel does, boldly developed with a hugeous spread to a glorious amplitude of swallowtail. His color was all that can well be desired, but ill described by any poor word palette. Enough that he seemed to tone away from olive and umber, with carmine stars, to glowing gold and soft pure silver, mantled with a subtle flush of rose and fawn and opal.

Swoop came a swallow, as we gazed, and was gone with a flick, having missed the May fly. But the wind of his passage, or the skir of wing, struck the merry dancer down, so that he fluttered for one instant on the wave, and that instant was enough. Swift as the swallow, and more true of aim, the great trout made one dart, and a sound, deeper than a tinkle, but as silvery as a bell, rang the poor ephemerid's knell. The rapid water scarcely showed a break; but a bubble sailed down the pool, and the dark hollow echoed with the music of a rise.

"He knows how to take a fly," said Pike; "he has had too many to be tricked with mine. Have him I must; but how ever shall I do it?"

All the way to Wellington he uttered not a word, but shambled along with a mind full of care. When I ventured to look up now and then, to surmise what was going on beneath his hat, deeply set eyes and a wrinkled forehead, relieved at long intervals by a solid shake, proved that there are meditations deeper than those of philosopher or statesman.

III

Surely no trout could have been misled by the artificial May fly of that time, unless he were either a very young fish, quite new to entomology, or else one afflicted with a combination of myopy and bulimy. Even now there is room for plenty of improvement in our counterfeit presentment; but in those days the body was made with yellow mohair, ribbed with red silk and gold twist and as thick as a fertile bumblebee. John Pike perceived that to offer such a thing to Crocker's trout would probably consign him—even if his great stamina should overget the horror—to an uneatable death, through just and natural indignation. On the other hand, while the May fly lasted, a trout so cultured, so highly refined, so full of light and sweetness, would never demean himself to low bait, or any coarse son of a maggot.

Meanwhile, Alec Bolt allowed poor Pike no peaceful thought, no calm absorption of high mind into the world of flies, no placid period of cobbler's wax, floss silk, turned hackles, and dubbing. For in making of flies John Pike had his special moments of inspiration, times of clearer insight into the everlasting verities, times of brighter conception and more subtle execution, tails of more elastic grace and heads of a neater and nattier expression. As a poet labors at one immortal line, compressing worlds of wisdom into the music of ten syllables, so toiled the patient Pike about the fabric of a fly comprising all the excellence that ever sprang from maggot. Yet Bolt rejoiced to jerk his elbow at the moment of sublimest art. And a swarm of flies was blighted thus.

Peaceful, therefore, and long-suffering, and full of resignation as he was, John Pike came slowly to the sad perception that arts avail not without arms. The elbow, so often jerked, at last took a voluntary jerk from the shoulder, and Alec Bolt lay prostrate, with his right eye full of cobbler's wax. This put a desirable check upon his energies for a week or more, and by that time Pike had flown his fly.

When the honeymoon of spring and summer (which they are now too fashionable to celebrate in this country), the heyday of the whole year marked by the budding of the wild rose, the start of the wheat ear from its sheath, the feathering of the lesser plantain, and flowering of the meadowsweet, and, foremost for the angler's joy, the caracole of May flies—when these things are to be seen and felt (which has not happened at all this year), then rivers should be mild and bright, skies blue and white with fleecy cloud, the west wind blowing softly, and the trout in charming appetite.

On such a day came Pike to the bank of Culm, with a loudly beating heart. A fly there is, not ignominious, or of cowdab origin, neither gross and heavy-bodied, from cradlehood of slimy stones, nor yet of menacing aspect and suggesting deeds of poison, but elegant, bland, and of sunny nature, and obviously good to eat. Him or her—why quest we which?—the shepherd of the dale, contemptuous of gender, except in his own species, has called, and as long as they two coexist will call, the Yellow Sally. A fly that does not waste the day in giddy dances and the fervid waltz, but undergoes family incidents with decorum and discretion. He or she, as the case may be—for the natural history of the riverbank is a book to come hereafter, and of fifty men who make flies not one knows

the name of the fly he is making—in the early morning of
June, or else in the second quarter of the afternoon, this Yellow
Sally fares aborad, with a nice well-ordered flutter.

Despairing of the May fly, as it still may be despaired of,
Pike came down to the river with his masterpiece of portrai-
ture. The artificial Yellow Sally is generally always—as they say
in Cheshire—a mile or more too yellow. On the other hand,
the Yellow Dun conveys no idea of any Sally. But Pike had
made a very decent Sally, not perfect (for he was young as well
as wise), but far above any counterfeit to be had in fishing-
tackle shops. How he made it, he told nobody. But if he lives
now, as I hope he does, any of my readers may ask him through
the G. P. O. and hope to get an answer.

It fluttered beautifully on the breeze, and in such living
form that a brother or sister Sally came up to see it, and went
away sadder and wiser. Then Pike said: "Get away, you young
wretch," to your humble servant who tells this tale; yet, being
better than his words, allowed that pious follower to lie down
upon his digestive organs and with deep attention watch.
There must have been great things to see, but to see them so
was difficult. And if I huddle up what happened, excitement
also shares the blame.

Pike had fashioned well the time and manner of this over-
ture. He knew that the giant Crockerite was satiate now with
May flies, or began to find their flavor failing, as happens to
us with asparagus, marrow-fat peas, or strawberries, when
we have had a month of them. And he thought that the first

Yellow Sally of the season, inferior though it were, might have the special charm of novelty. With the skill of a Zulu, he stole up through the branches over the lower pool till he came to a spot where a yard-wide opening gave just space for spring of rod. Then he saw his desirable friend at dinner, wagging his tail, as a hungry gentleman dining with the Lord Mayor agitates his coat. With one dexterous whirl, untaught by any of the many books upon the subject, John Pike laid his Yellow Sally (for he cast with one fly only) as lightly as gossamer upon the rapid, about a yard in front of the big trout's head. A moment's pause, and then too quick for words was the thing that happened.

A heavy plunge was followed by a fearful rush. Forgetful of the current the river was ridged, as if with a plow driven under it; the strong line, though given out as fast as might be, twanged like a harp string as it cut the wave, and then Pike stood up, like a ship dismasted, with the butt of his rod snapped below the ferrule. He had one of those foolish things, just invented, a hollow butt of hickory; and the finial ring of his spare top looked out, to ask what had happened to the rest of it. "Bad luck!" cried the fisherman; "but never mind, I shall have him next time, to a certainty."

When this great issue came to be considered, the cause of it was sadly obvious. The fish, being hooked, had made off with the rush of a shark for the bottom of the pool. A thicket of saplings below the alder tree had stopped the judicious hooker from all possibility of following; and when he strove to turn him by elastic pliance, his rod broke at the breach of pliability. "I have learned a sad lesson," said John Pike, looking sadly.

How many fellows would have given up this matter, and glorified themselves for having hooked so grand a fish, while explaining that they must have caught him, if they could have done it! But Pike only told me not to say a word about it, and began to make ready for another tug of war. He made himself a splice rod, short and handy, of well-seasoned ash, with a stout top of bamboo, tapered so discreetly, and so balanced in its spring, that verily it formed an arc, with any pressure on it, as perfect as a leafy poplar in a stormy summer. "Now break it if you can," he said, "by any amount of rushes; I'll hook you by your jacket collar; you cut away now, and I'll land you."

This was highly skillful, and he did it many times; and whenever I was landed well, I got a lollipop, so that I was careful not to break his tackle. Moreover he made him a landing net, with a kidney-bean stick, a ring of wire, and his own best nightcap of strong cotton net. Then he got the farmer's leave, and lopped obnoxious bushes; and now the chiefest question was: What bait, and when to offer it? In spite of his sad rebuff, the spirit of John Pike had been equable. The genuine angling mind is steadfast, large, and self-supported, and to the vapid, ignominious chaff, tossed by swine upon the idle wind, it pays as much heed as a big trout does to a dance of midges. People put their fingers to their noses and said: "Master Pike, have you caught him yet?" and Pike only answered: "Wait a bit." If ever this fortitude and perseverance is to be recovered as the

English Brand (the one thing that has made us what we are, and may yet redeem us from niddering shame), a degenerate age should encourage the habit of fishing and never despairing. And the brightest sign yet for our future is the increasing demand for hooks and gut.

Pike fished in a manlier age, when nobody would dream of cowering from a savage because he was clever at skulking; and when, if a big fish broke the rod, a stronger rod was made for him, according to the usage of Great Britain. And though the young angler had been defeated, he did not sit down and have a good cry over it.

About the second week in June, when the May fly had danced its day and died—for the season was an early one—and Crocker's trout had recovered from the wound to his feelings and philanthropy, there came a night of gentle rain, of pleasant tinkling upon window ledges, and a soothing patter among young leaves, and the Culm was yellow in the morning. "I mean to do it this afternoon," Pike whispered to me, as he came back panting. "When the water clears there will be a splendid time."

The lover of the rose knows well a gay voluptuous beetle, whose pleasure is to lie embedded in a fount of beauty. Deep among the incurving petals of the blushing fragrance, he loses himself in his joys sometimes, till a breezy waft reveals him. And when the sunlight breaks upon his luscious dissipation, few would have the heart to oust him, such a gem from such a setting. All his back is emerald sparkles, all his front red Indian gold, and here and there he grows white spots to save the eye from aching. Pike put his finger in and fetched him out, and offered him a little change of joys, by putting a Limerick hook through his thorax, and bringing it out between his elytra. *Cetonia aurata* liked it not, but pawed the air very naturally, and fluttered with his wings attractively.

"I meant to have tried with a fern web," said the angler; "until I saw one of these beggars this morning. If he works like that upon the water, he will do. It was hopeless to try artificials again. What a lovely color the water is! Only three days now to the holidays. I have run it very close. You be ready, younker."

With these words he stepped upon a branch of the alder, for the tone of the waters allowed approach, being soft and sublustrous, without any mud. Also Master Pike's own tone was such as becomes the fisherman, calm, deliberate, free from nerve, but full of eye and muscle. He stepped upon the alder bough to get as near as might be to the fish, for he could not cast this beetle like a fly; it must be dropped gently and allowed to play. "You may come and look," he said to me; "when the water is so, they have no eyes in their tails."

The rose beetle trod upon the water prettily, under a lively vibration, and he looked quite as happy and considerably more active, than when he had been cradled in the anthers of the rose. To the eye of a fish he was a strong individual, fighting courageously with the current, but sure to be beaten through lack of fins; and mercy suggested, as well as appetite, that the proper solution was to gulp him.

"Hooked him in the gullet. He can't get off!" cried John Pike, laboring to keep his nerves under. "Every inch of tackle is as strong as a bell pull. Now, if I don't land him, I will never fish again!"

Providence, which had constructed Pike, foremost of all things, for lofty angling—disdainful of worm and even minnow—Providence, I say, at this adjuration, pronounced that Pike must catch that trout. Not many anglers are heaven-born; and for one to drop off the hook halfway through his teens would be infinitely worse than to slay the champion trout. Pike felt the force of this, and rushing through the rushes, shouted: "I am sure to have him, Dick! Be ready with my nightcap."

Rod in a bow, like a springle riser; line on the hum, like the strong of Paganini; winch on the gallop, like a harpoon wheel, Pike, the headcenter of everything, dashing through thick and thin, and once taken overhead—for he jumped into the hole, when he must have lost him else, but the fish too impetuously towed him out, and made off in passion for another pool, when, if he had only retired to his hover, the angler might have shared the baker's fate—all these things (I tell you, for they all come upon again, as if the day were yesterday) so scared me of my never very steadfast wits, that I could only holloa! But one thing I did, I kept the nightcap ready.

The River Sneak

William Scrope

IF I WERE TO WRITE AN ACCOUNT OF HALF THE POACHING stories that are common to all Salmon rivers, I should produce a book, the dimensions of which would terrify the public, even in this pen-compelling age.

In times when water bailiffs in Tweed had very small salaries, they themselves were by no means scrupulous about the observance of close time, but partook of the good things of the river in all seasons, lawful or unlawful. There is a man now, I believe, living at Selkirk, who in times of yore used certain little freedoms with the Tweed Act, which did not become the virtue of his office. As a water bailiff he was sworn to tell of all he saw; and indeed, as he said, it could not be expected that he should tell of what he did not see.

When his dinner was served up during close time, his wife usually brought to the table in the first place a platter of potatoes and a napkin; she then bound the latter over his eyes that nothing might offend his sight. This being done, the illegal salmon was brought in smoking hot, and he fell to, blindfolded as he was, like a conscientious water bailiff,—if you know what that is; nor was the napkin taken from his eyes till the fins and bones were removed from the room, and every visible evidence of a salmon having been there had completely vanished: thus he saw no illegal act committed, and went to give in his annual report at Cornhill with his idea of a clear conscience. This was going too near the wind, or rather the water; but what would you have?—the man was literal, and a great eater of salmon from his youth.

People who are not water bailiffs have not always so delicate a conscience. Let us examine the style and bearing of such marauders as have fallen under our notice.

In the first place, there is your man with a pout net, which resembles a landing net, only that it is very considerably larger, and is in shape only half of a circle; with this he scoops out foul salmon during floods, when, from weakness, they are unable to stem the current, and get close under the banks. This he transacts very snugly, under pretence of taking trouts; so indeed he does, and welcome too, if he would stop there; but this he is perfectly averse from.

Next in consequence comes your Triton, who walks the waters with a long implement in his hands, namely a leister, alias a waster; with this weapon, "quocunque nomine gaudet," the said deity, quick of eye and ready of hand, forks out the poor fish that are spawning on the streams; and this in close time. Vile, vile Triton!

Then comes your lawless band of black fishers, so called from their masks of black crape with which they disguise themselves: these men come forth in the darkness of the night to burn for salmon. When the winds are hushed, you may sometimes hear the dipping of oars and the clanking of a boat chain, and see at a distance a small light, like a glow-worm. In a little while the light blazes forth, and up rise a set of Othellos who are about to take a private benefit. These minions of the night are generally men of a desperate character, and it is not easy to collect water bailiffs sufficient in number or willing to encounter them; but if water bailiffs would fight, how very picturesque the attack would be! The rapids,—the blazing,—the leisters,—the combatants driven headlong into the river. Why, the battle of Constantine and Maxentius, and the affair of the bridge, as seen in the famous fresco, would be nothing to it. The only thing I should apprehend would be, that the bailiffs would eventually sport Marc Antony and run.

In contradistinction to these illuminati comes your plausible poacher, a sort of river sneak. This man sallies forth with apparent innocence of purpose; he switches the water with a trout-rod, and ambulates the shore with a small basket at his back, indicative of humble pretensions; but has a pocket in his jacket that extends the whole breadth of the skirts. He is trouting, forsooth, but ever and anon, as he comes to a salmon-cast, he changes his fly, and has a go at the nobler animal. If he hooks a salmon, he looks on each side with the tail of his eye to guard against a surprise; and if he sees any danger of discovery from the advance of the foeman, he breaks his line, leaves the fly in the fish's mouth, and substitutes a trout one;—said fish swims away, and does not appear in evidence.

I once came upon one of these innocents, who had hold of a salmon with his trout-rod in a cast a little above Melrose bridge, called *"The Quarry Stream."* He did not see me, for I was in the copsewood on the summit of the bank immediately behind him. I could have pounced upon him at once, I and my fisherman. Did I do so? I tell you, no. He would have broken his line as above, and have lost the fish; and I wanted a salmon, for it is a delicate animal, and was particularly scarce at that time.

So I desired Charlie to lie down amongst the bushes, and not to stir till the fish was fairly landed, and was in the capacious pocket, which has already been described. Then I counselled him to give chase, and harry the possessor. Judging, however, that if the man crossed the river at the ford a little below, which he was very likely to do, that he would have so much law of Charlie before he could descend the steep brae, that he might escape: I drew back cautiously, got into the road out of sight, and passed over Melrose bridge, taking care to bend my body so as to keep it out of sight behind the parapet; I then lay concealed amongst the firs in the opposite bank. Thus we had Master Sneak between us. I was at some distance from the scene of action to be sure, and somewhat in the rear, as I could advance no further under cover; but I had the upper ground, and was tolerably swift of foot in those days, which gave me confidence. I took out my pocket glass, and eyed my man. He was no novice: but worked his fish with great skill. At length he drew him on the shore, and gave him a settler with a rap of a stone on the back of his head; he then, honest man, pryed around him with great circumspection, and seeing no one, he took the salmon by the tail, and, full of internal contentment, deposited it in his well-contrived pocket: he then waded across to the south side of the river, with an intention, as it seemed, of revisiting his household gods and having a broil.

Charlie now arose from his lair, and scrambled down the steep. The alarm was given, but he of the salmon had a good start, with the river between him and his pursuer. So he stopped for a moment on the haugh to make out what was going forward on all sides, much after the fashion of an old hare, who runs a certain distance when she apprehends any thing personal, then rests for a moment or two, and shifts her ears in order to collect the news from all quarters of the compass. Even so did our friend, and having satisfied himself that he was a favoured object of attraction, he was coy, and took to flight incontinently; I now sprang up from the firs, the game being fairly afoot, and kept the upper ground. The pursuit became close and hot, but as the fugitive, like Johnny Gilpin, carried weight, I soon closed with him.

"You seem in a hurry, my good friend, your business must be pressing. What makes you run so?"

"Did ye no see that bogle there by the quarry stream, that garred me rin this gait, haud on for yer lives, sirs, for if he overtakes us, we are deid men."

"Why, the truth is, Sandy, that I do not choose to haud on at present, because I came forth in quest of a bonny salmon, and cannot go home without one; could you not help me to such a thing?"

At this Sandy took a pinch of snuff from his mull, and seeing my eyes fixed upon the length and protuberance of his pocket, answered quaintly enough,—

"Aye, that can I, and right glad am I to do ye a favour, ye shall no want for a salmon whilst I have one."

So saying, he pulled forth a ten pounder, which occupied all the lower regions of his jacket. "How the beast got here," said he, as he extracted him gradually, "I dinna ken, but I am thinking that he must have louped intill my pocket, as I war wading the river."

"Nothing more likely, and I will admit him to have done so for once, but, mark me, I will not admit of any salmon doing so in future without my permission in writing. You have been trouting, it seems, pray what sort of a fly do you use?"

"Whiles I use a wee ane, and while a muckle flee, ane for rough and deep water, and the ither for shallow streams. That is the way to trout, both in loch and river."

"True! I see you have some bonny little flies in your hat; take it off carefully, Purdie—you understand me,—and let me admire them."

Charlie advances, and taking off the man's hat with great care so as to keep the crown undermost, he pulls out from the inside six well tied salmon flies of the most approved colours, which he transferred to his own pocket. I actually saw *"Meg with the muckle mouth"* amongst them.

"Aye, ye are as welcome to the flees as ye are to the sawmont, and I am proud to do ye a good turn at ony gait."

"Well now, bear in mind, that I will never permit you to throw a fly wee or muckle in the Pavilion-water again; and if you darken the shores with your presence a second time, I will have you up at Melrose."

"I'm thinking I shall tak' your advice, for ye seem a sensible chiel. Will ye accept a pinch of snuff?"

"Good morning, good morning, get home to. Selkirk as quick as ye can; we know ye well for a souter of that town. Run, run, the bogle is after you!"

"Run, aye that will I, and the deil tak' the hindmost," said he, and off he went at his best pace; leaving this blessing and the salmon to solace us.

Fishing with a Worm

Bliss Perry

BELOW THE LOWER ROAD THE TAYLOR BROOK BECOMES uncertain water. For half a mile it yields only fingerlings, for no explainable reason; then there are two miles of clean fishing through the deep woods, where the branches are so high that you can cast a fly again if you like, and there are long pools, where now and then a heavy fish will rise; then comes a final half mile through the alders, where you must wade, knee to waist deep, before you come to the bridge and the river. Glorious fishing is sometimes to be had here, especially if you work down the gorge at twilight, casting a white miller until it is too dark to see. But alas, there is a well-worn path along the brook, and often enough there are the very footprints of the fellow ahead of you, signs as disheartening to the fisherman as ever were the footprints on the sand to Robinson Crusoe.

But "between the roads" it is "too much trouble to fish;" and there lies the salvation of the humble fisherman who disdains not to use the crawling worm, nor, for that matter, to crawl himself, if need be, in order to sneak under the boughs of some overhanging cedar that casts a perpetual shadow upon the sleepy brook. Lying here at full length, with no elbow room to manage the rod, you must occasionally even unjoint your tip and fish with that, using but a dozen inches of line, and not letting so much as your eyebrows show above the bank. Is it a becoming attitude for a middle-aged citizen of the world? That depends upon how the fish are biting. Holing a putt looks rather ridiculous also, to the mere observer, but it requires, like brook fishing with a tip only, a very delicate wrist, perfect tactile sense, and a fine disregard of appearances.

There are some fishermen who always fish as if they were being photographed. The Taylor Brook "between the roads" is not for them. To fish it at all is back-breaking, trouser-tearing work; to see it thoroughly fished is to learn new lessons in the art of angling.

To watch R., for example, steadily filling his six-pound creel from that unlikely stream is like watching Sargent paint a portrait. R. weighs two hundred and ten. Twenty years ago he was a famous amateur pitcher, and among his present avocations are violin playing, which is good for the wrist, taxidermy, which is good for the eye, and shooting woodcock, which before the days of the new Nature Study used to be thought good for the whole man. R. began as a fly-fisherman, but by dint of passing his summers near brooks where fly-fishing is impossible, he has become a stout-hearted apologist for the worm. His apparatus is most singular. It consists of a very long, cheap rod, stout enough to smash through bushes, and with the stiffest tip obtainable. The lower end of the butt, below the reel, fits into the socket of a huge extra butt of bamboo, which R. carries unconcernedly. To reach a distant hole, or to fish the lower end of a ripple, R. simply locks his reel, slips on the extra butt, and there is a fourteen-foot rod ready for action. He fishes with a line unbelievably short, and a Kendal hook far too big; and when a trout jumps for that hook, R. wastes no time in manoeuvring for position. The unlucky fish is simply "derricked" to borrow a word from Theodore, most saturnine and profane of Moosehead guides.

"Shall I play him awhile?" shouted an excited sportsman to Theodore, after hooking his first big trout.

"———no!" growled Theodore in disgust. "Just derrick him right into the canoe!" An heroic method, surely; though it once cost me the best squaretail I ever hooked, for Theodore had forgotten the landing net, and the gut broke in his fingers as he tried to swing the fish abroad. But with these lively quarter-pounders of the Taylor Brook, derricking is a safer procedure. Indeed, I have sat dejectedly on the far end of a log, after fishing the hole under it in vain, and seen the mighty R. wade downstream close behind me, adjust that comical extra butt, and jerk a couple of half-pound trout from under the very log on which I was sitting. His device on this occasion, as I well remember, was to pass his hook but once through the middle of a big worm, let the worm sink to the bottom and crawl along it at his leisure. The trout could not resist.

Once, and once only, have I come near equaling R.'s record, and the way he beat me then is the justification for a whole philosophy of worm-fishing. We were on this very Taylor Brook, and at five in the afternoon both baskets were two thirds full. By count I had just one more fish than he. It was raining hard.

"You fish down through the alders," said R. magnanimously. "I'll cut across and wait for you at the sawmill. I don't want to get any wetter, on account of my rheumatism."

This was rather barefaced kindness—for whose rheumatism was ever the worse for another hour's fishing? But I weakly accepted it. I coveted three or four good trout to top off with—that was all. So I tied on a couple of flies and began to fish the alders, wading waist-deep in the rapidly rising water, down the long green tunnel under the curving boughs. The brook fairly smoked with the rain, by this time, but when did one fail to get at least three or four trout out of his best half mile of the lower brook? Yet I had no luck. I tried one fly after another, and then, as a forlorn hope,—though it sometimes has a magic of its own,—I combined a brown hackle for the tail fly with a twisting worm on the dropper. Not a rise!

I thought of R. sitting patiently in the sawmill, and I fished more conscientiously than ever.

> *Venture as warily, use the same skill,*
> *Do your best, whether winning or losing it,*
> *If you choose to play!—is my principle.*

Even those lines, which by some subtle telepathy of the trout brook murmur themselves over and over to me in the waning hours of an unlucky day, brought now no consolation.

There was simply not one fish to be had, to any fly in the book, out of that long, drenching, darkening tunnel. At last I climbed out of the brook, by the bridge. R. was sitting on the fence, his neck and ears carefully turtled under his coat collar, the smoke rising and the rain dripping from the inverted bowl of his pipe. He did not seem to be worrying about his rheumatism.

"What luck?" he asked.

"None at all," I answered morosely. "Sorry to keep you waiting."

"That's all right," remarked R. "What do you think I've been doing? I've been fishing out of the sawmill window just to kill time. There was a patch of floating sawdust there,—kind of unlikely place for trout, anyway,—but I thought I'd put on a worm and let him crawl around a little." He opened his creel as he spoke.

"But I didn't look for a pair of 'em," he added. And there, on top of his smaller fish, were as pretty a pair of three-quarter-pound brook trout as were ever basketed.

"I'm afraid you got pretty wet," said R. kindly.

"I don't mind that," I replied. And I didn't. What I minded was the thought of an hour's vain wading in that roaring stream whipping it with fly after fly, while R., the foreordained fisherman, was sitting comfortably in a sawmill, and derricking that pair of three-quarter-pounds in through the window! I had ventured more warily than he, and used, if not the same skill, at least the best skill at my command. My conscience was clear, but so was his; and he had had the drier skin and the greater magnanimity and the biggest fish besides. There is much to be said, in a world like ours, for taking the world as you find it and for fishing with a worm.

The Angler

Washington Irving

IT IS SAID THAT MANY AN UNLUCKY URCHIN IS INDUCED TO run away from his family and betake himself to a seafaring life, from reading the history of Robinson Crusoe; and I suspect that, in like manner, many of those worthy gentlemen who are given to haunt the sides of pastoral streams with angle rods in hand, may trace the origin of their passion to the seductive pages of honest Izaak Walton. I recollect studying his *Compleat Angler* several years since, in company with a knot of friends in America, and moreover that we were all completely bitten with the angling mania. It was early in the year; but as soon as the weather was auspicious, and that the spring began to melt into the verge of summer, we took rod in hand and sallied into the country, as stark mad as was ever Don Quixote from reading books of chivalry.

One of our party had equalled the Don in the fullness of his equipments; being attired *cap-à-pie* for the enterprise. He wore a broad-skirted fustian coat, perplexed with half a hundred pockets; a pair of stout shoes and leathern gaiters; a basket slung on one side for fish; a patent rod, a landing-net, and a score of other inconveniences, only to be found in the true angler's armoury. Thus harnessed for the field, he was as great a matter of stare and wonderment among the country folk, who had never seen a regular angler, as was the steel-clad hero of La Mancha among the goatherds of the Sierra Morena.

Our first essay was along a mountain brook, among the highlands of the Hudson; a most unfortunate place for the execution of those piscatory tactics which had been invented along the velvet margins of quiet English rivulets. It was one of those wild streams that lavish, among our romantic solitudes, unheeded beauties, enough to fill the sketch book of a hunter of the picturesque. Sometimes it would leap down rocky shelves, making small cascades, over which the trees threw their broad balancing sprays, and long nameless weeds hung in fringes from the impending banks, dripping with diamond drops. Sometimes it would brawl and fret along a ravine in the matted shade of a forest, filling it with murmurs; and, after this termagant career, would steal forth into open day with the most placid demure face imaginable; as I have seen some pestilent shrew of a housewife, after filling her home with uproar and ill-humour, come dimpling out of doors, swimming and courtseying, and smiling upon all the world.

How smoothly would this vagrant brook glide, at such times, through some bosom of green meadow-land among the mountains; where the quiet was only interrupted by the occasional tinkling of a bell from the lazy cattle among the

clover, or the sound of a woodcutter's axe from the neighbouring forest.

For my part, I was always a bungler at all kinds of sport
that required either patience or adroitness, and had not angled
above half an hour before I had completely "satisfied the sentiment," and convinced myself of the truth of Izaak Walton's
opinion, that angling is something like poetry—a man must be
born to it. I hooked myself instead of the fish; tangled my line
in every tree; lost my bait; broke my rod; until I gave up the
attempt in despair, and passed the day under the trees, reading
old Izaak; satisfied that it was his fascinating vein of honest
simplicity and rural feeling that had bewitched me, and not the
passion for angling. My companions, however, were more per-
severing in their delusion. I have them at this moment before
my eyes, stealing along the border of the brook, where it lay
open to the day, or was merely fringed by shrubs and bushes.
I see the bittern rising with hollow scream as they break in
upon his rarely invaded haunt; the kingfisher watching them
suspiciously from his dry tree that overhangs the deep black
millpond, in the gorge of the hills; the tortoise letting himself
slip sideways from off the stone or log on which he is sunning
himself; and the panic-struck frog plumping in headlong as
they approach, and spreading an alarm throughout the watery
world around.

I recollect also, that, after toiling and watching and creeping about for the greater part of a day, with scarcely any success, in spite of all our admirable apparatus, a lubberly country

urchin came down from the hills with a rod made from a branch of a tree, a few yards of twine, and, as Heaven shall help me! I believe a crooked pin for a hook, baited with a vile earthworm—and in half an hour caught more fish than we had nibbles throughout the day!

But, above all, I recollect the "good, honest, wholesome, hungry" repast, which we made under a beech-tree, just by a spring of pure sweet water that stole out of the side of a hill; and how, when it was over, one of the party read old Izaak Walton's scene with the milkmaid, while I lay on the grass and built castles in a bright pile of clouds, until I fell asleep. All this may appear like mere egotism; yet I cannot refrain from utter-ing these recollections, which are passing like a strain of music over my mind, and have been called up by an agreeable scene which I witnessed not long since.

In a morning stroll along the banks of Alun, a beauti-ful little stream which flows down from the Welsh hills, and throws itself into the Dee, my attention was attracted to a group seated on the margin. On approaching, I found it to consist of a veteran angler and two rustic disciples. The for-mer was an old fellow with a wooden leg, with clothes very much but very carefully patched, betokening poverty, honestly come by, and decently maintained. His face bore the marks of former storms, but present fair weather; its furrows had been worn into an habitual smile; his iron-gray locks hung about his ears, and he had altogether the good-humoured air of a constitutional philosopher who was disposed to take the world as it went. One of his companions was a ragged wight, with the skulking look of an arrant poacher, and I'll warrant could find his way to any gentleman's fish-pond in the neighbourhood in the darkest night. The other was a tall, awkward, country lad, with a lounging gait, and apparently somewhat of a rustic beau. The old man was busy in examining the maw of a trout which he had just killed, to discover by its contents what insects were seasonable for bait; and was lecturing on the subject to his companions, who appeared to listen with infinite deference. I have a kind feeling towards all "brothers of the angle," ever since I read Izaak Walton. They are men, he affirms, of a "mild, sweet, and peaceable spirit"; and my esteem for them has been increased since I met with an old *Tretyse of fishing with the Angle*, in which are set forth many of the maxims of their inoffensive fraternity. "Take good hede," sayeth this honest little tretyse, "that in going about your disportes ye open no man's gates, but that ye shet them again. Also ye shall not use this forsayd crafti disport for no covetousness to the encreasing and sparing of your money only, but principally for your solace, and to cause the helth of your body and specyally of your soule."

I thought that I could perceive in the veteran angler before me an exemplification of what I had read; and there was a cheerful contentedness in his looks that quite drew me towards him. I could not but remark the gallant manner in which he stumped from one part of the brook to another; waving his rod in the air, to keep the line from dragging on the ground, or catching among the bushes; and the adroitness with which he would throw his fly to any particular place; sometimes skimming it lightly along a little rapid; sometimes casting it into one of those dark holes made by a twisted root or overhanging bank, in which the large trout are apt to lurk. In the meanwhile he was giving instructions to his two disciples; showing them the manner in which they should handle their rods, fix their flies, and play them along the surface of the stream. The scene brought to my mind the instruction of the sage Piscator to his scholar. The country around was of that pastoral kind which Walton is fond of describing. It was a part of the great plain of Cheshire, close by the beautiful vale of Gessford, and just where the inferior Welsh hills begin to swell up from among fresh-smelling meadows. The day, too, like that recorded in his work, was mild and sunshiny, with now and then a soft-dropping shower, that sowed the whole earth with diamonds.

I soon fell into conversation with the old angler, and was so much entertained, that, under pretext of receiving instructions in his art, I kept company with him almost the whole day; wandering along the banks of the stream, and listening to his talk. He was very communicative, having all the easy garrulity of cheerful old age; and I fancy was a little flattered by having an opportunity of displaying his piscatory lore; for who does not like now and then to play the sage?

He had been much of a rambler in his day, and had passed some years of his youth in America, particularly in Savannah, where he had entered into trade and had been ruined by the indiscretion of a partner. He had afterwards experienced many ups and downs in life, until he got into the navy, where his leg was carried away by a cannon-ball, at the battle of Camperdown. This was the only stroke of real good fortune he had ever experienced, for it got him a pension, which, together with some small paternal property brought him in a revenue of nearly forty pounds. On this he retired to his native village where he lived quietly and independently; and devoted the remainder of his life to the "noble art of angling."

I found that he had read Izaak Walton attentively, and he seemed to have imbibed all his simple frankness and prevalent good humour. Though he had been sorely buffeted about the world, he was satisfied that the world, in itself, was good and beautiful. Though he had been as roughly used in different countries as a poor sheep that is fleeced by every hedge and thicket, yet he spoke of every nation with candour and kindness, appearing to look only on the good side of things; and, above all, he was almost the only man I had ever met with who had been an unfortunate adventurer in America and had honesty and magnanimity enough to take the fault to his own door, and not to curse the country. The lad that was receiving his instructions, I learnt, was the son and heir apparent of a fat old widow who kept the village inn, and of course a youth of some expectation, and much courted by the idle gentleman-like personages of the place. In taking him under his care, therefore, the old man had probably an eye to a privileged corner in the taproom, and an occasional cup of cheerful ale free of expense.

There is certainly something in angling, if we could forget, which anglers are apt to do, the cruelties and tortures inflicted on worms and insects, that tends to produce a gentleness of spirit, and a pure serenity of mind. As the English are methodical, even in their recreations, and are the most scientific of sportsmen, it has been reduced among them to perfect rule and system. Indeed, it is an amusement peculiarly adapted to the mild and highly cultivated scenery of England, where every roughness has been softened away from the landscape. It is delightful to saunter along those limpid streams which wander, like veins of silver, through the bosom of this beautiful country; leading one through a diversity of small home scenery; sometimes winding through ornamented grounds; sometimes brimming along through rich pasturage, where the fresh green is mingled with sweet-smelling flowers; sometimes venturing in sight of villages and hamlets, and then running capriciously away into shady retirements. The sweetness and serenity of nature, and the quiet watchfulness of the sport, gradually bring on pleasant fits of musing, which are now and then agreeably interrupted by the song of a bird, the distant whistle of the peasant, or perhaps the vagary of some fish, leaping out of the still water, and skimming transiently about its glassy surface. "When I would beget content," says Izaak Walton, "and increase confidence in the power and wisdom and providence of Almighty God, I will walk the meadows by some gliding stream, and there contemplate the lilies that take no care, and those very many other little living creatures that are not only created, but feed (man knows not how) by the goodness of the God of nature, and therefore trust in him."

I cannot forbear to give another quotation from one of those ancient champions of angling, which breathes the same innocent and happy spirit:

> *Let me live harmlessly, and near the brink*
> *Of Trent or Avon have a dwelling-place,*
> *Where I may see my quill, or cork, down sink,*
> *With eager bite of pike, or bleak, or dace;*
> *And on the world and my Creator think:*
> *Whilst some men strive ill-gotten goods t' embrace;*
> *And others spend their time in base excess*
> *Of wine, or worse, in war, or wantonness.*
> *Let them that will, these pastimes still pursue,*
> *And on such pleasing fancies feed their fill;*
> *So I the fields and meadows green may view,*
> *And daily by fresh rivers walk at will,*
> *Among the daisies and the violets blue,*
> *Red hyacinth and yellow daffodil.*

On parting with the old angler, I inquired after his place of abode, and happening to be in the neighbourhood of the village a few evenings afterwards, I had the curiosity to seek him out. I found him living in a small cottage, containing only one room, but a perfect curiosity in its method and arrangement. It was on the skirts of the village, on a green bank, a little back from the road, with a small garden in front, stocked with kitchen herbs, and adorned with a few flowers. The whole front of the cottage was overrun with a honeysuckle. On the top was a ship for a weathercock. The interior was fitted up in a truly nautical style, his ideas of comfort and convenience having been acquired on the berth-deck of a man-of-war. A hammock was slung from the ceiling, which, in the daytime, was lashed up so as to take but little room. From the centre of the chamber hung a model of a ship, of his own workmanship. Two or three chairs, a table, and a large sea-chest, formed the principal moveables. About the wall were stuck up naval ballads, such as "Admiral Hosier's Ghost," "All in the Downs," and "Tom Bowling," intermingled with pictures of sea-fights, among which the battle of Camperdown held a distinguished place. The mantlepiece was decorated with sea-shells, over which hung a quadrant, flanked by two wood-cuts of most bitter-looking naval commanders. His implements for angling were carefully disposed on nails and hooks about the room. On a shelf was arranged his library, containing a work on angling, much worn, a Bible covered with canvas, an odd volume or two of voyages, a nautical almanack, and a book of songs.

His family consisted of a large black cat with one eye, and a parrot which he had caught and tamed, and educated himself, in the course of one of his voyages; and which uttered a variety of sea phrases with the hoarse brattling tone of a veteran boatswain. The establishment reminded me of that of the renowned Robinson Crusoe; it was kept in neat order, everything being "stowed away" with the regularity of a ship of war; and he informed me that he "scoured the deck every morning, and swept it between meals."

I found him seated on a bench before the door, smoking his pipe in the soft evening sunshine. His cat was purring soberly on the threshold, and his parrot describing some strange evolutions in an iron ring that swung in the centre of his cage. He had been angling all day, and gave me a history of his sport with as much minuteness as a general would talk over a campaign; being particularly animated in relating the manner in which he had taken a large trout, which had completely tasked all his skill and wariness, and which he had sent as a trophy to mine hostess of the inn.

How comforting it is to see a cheerful and contented old age; and to behold a poor fellow, like this, after being tempest-tost through life, safely moored in a snug and quiet harbour in the evening of his days! His happiness, however, sprung from within himself, and was independent of external circumstances; for he had that inexhaustible good nature, which is the most precious gift of Heaven; spreading itself like oil over the troubled sea of thought, and keeping the mind smooth and equable in the roughest weather.

On inquiring further about him, I learnt that he was a universal favourite in the village, and the oracle of the taproom; where he delighted the rustics with his songs, and, like Sinbad, astonished them with his stories of strange lands, and shipwrecks, and sea-fights. He was much noticed, too, by gentlemen sportsmen of the neighbourhood; had taught several of them the art of angling; and was a privileged visitor to their kitchens. The whole tenor of his life was quiet, and inoffensive, being principally passed about the neighbouring streams, when the weather and season were favourable; and at other times he employed himself at home, preparing his fishing tackle for the next campaign, or manufacturing rods, nets, and flies, for his patrons and pupils among the gentry.

He was a regular attendant at church on Sundays, though he generally fell asleep during the sermon. He had made it his particular request that when he died he should be buried in a green spot, which he could see from his seat in church, and which he had marked out ever since he was a boy, and had thought of when far from home on the raging sea, in danger of being food for the fishes—it was the spot where his father and mother had been buried.

I have done, for I fear that my reader is growing weary; but I could not refrain from drawing the picture of this worthy "brother of the angle"; who has made me more than ever in love with the theory, though I fear I shall never be adroit in the practice, of his art; and I will conclude this rambling sketch in the words of honest Izaak Walton, by craving the blessing of St. Peter's master upon my reader, "and upon all that are true lovers of virtue; and dare trust in his providence: and be quiet; and go a angling."

Story-Telling on the Thames

Jerome K. Jerome

THE NEIGHBOURHOOD OF STREATLEY AND GORING IS A GREAT fishing centre. There is some excellent fishing to be had here. The river abounds in pike, roach, dace, gudgeon, and eels, just here; and you can sit and fish for them all day.

Some people do. They never catch them. I never knew anybody catch anything, up the Thames, except minnows and dead cats, but that has nothing to do, of course, with fishing! The local fisherman's guide doesn't say a word about catching anything. All it says is the place is "a good station for fishing;" and, from what I have seen of the district, I am quite prepared to bear out this statement.

There is no spot in the world where you can get more fishing, or where you can fish for a longer period. Some fishermen come here and fish for a day, and others stop and fish for a month. You can hang on and fish for a year, if you want to; it will be all the same.

The Angler's Guide to the Thames says that "jack and perch are also to be had about here," but there the *Angler's Guide* is wrong. Jack and perch may be about there. Indeed, I know for a fact that they are. You can see them there in shoals, when you are out for a walk along the banks: they come and stand half out of the water with their mouths open for biscuits. And, if you go for a bathe, they crowd round, and get in your way, and irritate you. But they are not to be "had" by a bit of worm on the end of a hook, nor anything like it—not they!

I am not a good fisherman myself. I devoted a considerable amount of attention to the subject at one time, and was getting on, as I thought, fairly well; but the old hands told me that I should never be any real good at it, and advised me to give it up. They said that I was an extremely neat thrower, and that I seemed to have plenty of gumption for the thing, and quite enough constitutional laziness. But they were sure I should never make anything of a fisherman. I had not got sufficient imagination.

They said that as a poet, or a shilling shocker, or a report, or anything of that kind, I might be satisfactory, but that, to gain any position as a Thames angler, would require more play of fancy, more power of invention than I appeared to possess.

Some people are under the impression that all that is required to make a good fisherman is the ability to tell lies easily and without blushing; but this is a mistake. Mere bald fabrication is useless; the veriest tyro can manage that. It is in the circumstantial detail, the embellishing touches of probability, the general air of scrupulous—almost of pedantic—veracity, that the experienced angler is seen.

Anybody can come in and say, "Oh, I caught fifteen dozen perch yesterday evening;" or "Last Monday I landed a gudgeon, weighing eighteen pounds, and measuring three feet from the tip to the tail."

There is no art, no skill, required for that sort of thing. It shows pluck, but that is all.

No; your accomplished angler would scorn to tell a lie, that way. His method is a study in itself.

He comes in quietly with his hat on, appropriates the most comfortable chair, lights his pipe, and commences to puff in silence. He lets the youngsters brag away for a while, and then, during a momentary lull, he removes the pipe from his mouth, and remarks, as he knocks the ashes out against the bars:

"Well, I had a haul on Tuesday evening that it's not much good my telling anybody about."

"Oh! why's that?" they ask.

"Because I don't expect anybody would believe me if I did," replies the old fellow calmly, and without even a tinge of bitterness in his tone, as he refills his pipe, and requests the landlord to bring him three of Scotch,—cold.

There is a pause after this, nobody feeling sufficiently sure of himself to contradict the old gentleman. So he has to go on by himself without any encouragement.

"No," he continues thoughtfully; "I shouldn't believe it myself if anybody told it to me, but it's a fact, for all that. I had been sitting there all the afternoon and had caught literally nothing—except a few dozen dace and a score of jack;

and I was just about giving it up as a bad job when I suddenly felt a rather smart pull at the line. I thought it was another little one, and I went to jerk it up. Hang me, if I could move the rod! It took me half-an-hour—half-an-hour, sir!—to land that fish; and every moment I thought the line was going to snap! I reached him at last, and what do you think it was? A sturgeon! a forty pound sturgeon! taken on a line, sir! Yes, you may well look surprised—I'll have another three of Scotch, landlord, please."

And then he goes on to tell of the astonishment of everybody who saw it; and what his wife said, when he got home, and of what Joe Buggles thought about it.

I asked the landlord of an inn up the river once, if it did not injure him, sometimes, listening to the tales that the fishermen about there told him; and he said:

"Oh, no; not now, sir. It did used to knock me over a bit at first, but, lor love you! me and the missus we listens to 'em all day now. It's what you're used to, you know. It's what you're used to."

I knew a young man once, he was a most conscientious fellow, and, when he took to fly-fishing, he determined never to exaggerate his hauls by more than twenty-five per cent.

"When I have caught forty fish," said he, "then I will tell people that I have caught fifty, and so on. But I will not lie any more than that, because it is sinful to lie."

But the twenty-five per cent plan did not work well at all. He never was able to use it. The greatest number of fish he ever caught in one day was three, and you can't add twenty-five per cent to three—at least, not in fish.

So he increased his percentage to thirty-three and a third; but that, again, was awkward, when he had only caught one or two; so, to simplify matters, he made up his mind to just double the quantity.

He stuck to this arrangement for a couple of months, and then he grew dissatisfied with it. Nobody believed him when he told them that he only doubled, and he, therefore, gained no credit that way whatever, while his moderation put him at a disadvantage among the other anglers. When he had really caught three small fish, and said he had six, it used to make him quite jealous to hear a man, whom he knew for a fact had only caught one, going about telling people he had landed two dozen.

So, eventually, he made one final arrangement with himself, which he has religiously held to ever since, and that was to count each fish that he caught as ten, and to assume ten to begin with. For example, if he did not catch any fish at all, then he said he had caught ten fish—you could never catch less than ten fish by his system; that was the foundation of it. Then, if by any chance he really did catch one fish, he called it twenty, while two fish would count thirty, three forty, and so on.

It is a simple and easily worked plan, and there has been some talk lately of its being made use of by the angling fraternity in general. Indeed, the Committee of the Thames Angler's

Association did recommend its adoption about two years ago, but some of the older members opposed it. They said they would consider the idea if the number were doubled, and each fish counted as twenty.

If ever you have an evening to spare, up the river, I should advise you to drop into one of the little village inns, and take a seat in the tap-room. You will be nearly sure to meet one or two old rod-men, sipping their toddy there, and they will tell you enough fishy stories, in half an hour, to give you indigestion for a month.

George and I—I don't know what had become of Harris; he had gone out and had a shave, early in the afternoon, and had then come back and spent full forty minutes in pipeclaying his shoes, we had not seen him since—George and I, therefore, and the dog, left to ourselves, went for a walk to Wallingford on the second evening, and, coming home, we called in at a little river-side inn, for a rest, and other things.

We went into the parlour and sat down. There was an old fellow there, smoking a long clay pipe, and we naturally began chatting.

He told us that it had been a fine day to-day, and we told him that it had been a fine day yesterday, and then we all told each other that we thought it would be a fine day to-morrow; and George said the crops seemed to be coming up nicely.

After that it came out, somehow or other, that we were strangers in the neighbourhood, and that we were going away the next morning.

Then a pause ensued in the conversation, during which our eyes wandered round the room. They finally rested upon a dusty old glass-case, fixed very high up above the chimney-piece, and containing a trout. It rather fascinated me, that trout; it was such a monstrous fish. In fact, at first glance, I thought it was a cod.

"Ah!" said the old gentleman, following the direction of my gaze, "fine fellow that, ain't he?"

"Quite uncommon," I murmured; and George asked the old man how much he thought it weighed.

"Eighteen pounds six ounces," said our friend, rising and taking down his coat. "Yes," he continued, "it wur sixteen year ago, come the third o' next month, that I landed him. I caught him just below the bridge with a minnow. They told me he wur in the river, and I said I'd have him, and so I did. You don't see many fish that size about here now, I'm thinking. Good-night, gentlemen, good-night."

And out he went, and left us alone.

We could not take our eyes off the fish after that. It really was a remarkably fine fish. We were still looking at it, when the local carrier, who had just stopped at the inn, came to the door of the room with a pot of beer in his hand, and he also looked at the fish.

"Good-sized trout, that," said George, turning round to him.

"Ah! you may well say that, sir," replied the man; and then, after a pull at his beer, he added, "Maybe you wasn't here, sir, when that fish was caught?"

"No," we told him. We were strangers in the neighbourhood.

"Ah!" said the carrier, "then, of course, how should you? It was nearly five years ago that I caught that trout."

"Oh! was it you who caught it, then?" said I.

"Yes, sir," replied the genial old fellow. "I caught him just below the lock—leastways, what was the lock then—one Friday afternoon; and the remarkable thing about it is that I caught him with a fly. I'd gone out pike fishing, bless you, never thinking of a trout, and when I saw that whopper on the end of my line, blest if it didn't quite take me aback. Well, you see, he weighed twenty-six pound. Good-night, gentlemen, good-night."

Five minutes afterwards, a third man came in, and described how *he* had caught it early one morning, with bleak; and then he left, and a stolid, solemn-looking, middle-aged individual came in, and sat down over by the window.

None of us spoke for a while; but at length, George turned to the new comer, and said:

"I beg your pardon, I hope you will forgive the liberty that we—perfect strangers in the neighbourhood—are taking, but my friend here and myself would be much obliged if you would tell us how you caught that trout."

"Why, who told you I caught that trout!" was the surprised query.

We said that nobody had told us so, but somehow or other we felt instinctively that it was he who had done it.

"Well, it's a most remarkable thing—most remarkable,"

answered the stolid stranger, laughing; "because, as a matter of fact, you are quite right. I did catch it. But fancy your guessing it like that. Dear me, it's really a most remarkable thing."

And then he went on, and told us how it had taken him half an hour to land it, and how it had broke his rod. He said he had weighed it carefully when he reached home, and it had turned the scale at thirty-four pounds.

He went in his turn, and when he was gone, the landlord came in to us. We told him the various histories we had heard about his trout, and he was immensely amused, and we all laughed very heartily.

"Fancy Jim Bates and Joe Muggles and Mr. Jones and old Billy Maunders all telling you that they had caught it. Ha! ha! ha! Well, that is good," said the honest old fellow, laughing heartily. "Yes, they are the sort to give it to *me*, to put up in *my* parlour, if *they* had caught it, they are! Ha! ha! ha!"

And then he told us the real history of the fish. It seemed that he had caught it himself, years ago, when he was quite a lad; not by any art or skill, but by that unaccountable luck that appears to always wait upon a boy when he plays the wag from school, and goes way out fishing on a sunny afternoon, with a bit of string tied on to the end of a tree.

He said that bringing home that trout had saved him from a whacking, and that even his schoolmaster had said it was worth the rule-of-three and practice put together.

He was called out of the room at this point, and George and I again turned our gaze upon the fish.

It really was a most astonishing trout. The more we looked at it, the more we marvelled at it.

It excited George so much that he climbed up on the back of a chair to get a better view of it.

And then the chair slipped, and George clutched wildly at the trout-case to save himself, and down it came with a crash, George and the chair on top of it.

"You haven't injured the fish, have you?" I cried in alarm, rushing up.

"I hope not," said George, rising cautiously and looking about.

But he had. That trout lay shattered into a thousand fragments—I say a thousand, but they may have only been nine hundred. I did not count them.

We thought it strange and unaccountable that a stuffed trout should break up into little pieces like that.

And so it would have been strange and unaccountable, if it had been a stuffed trout, but it was not.

That trout was plaster-of-Paris.

A Fishing Excursion

Guy de Maupassant

PARIS WAS BLOCKADED, DESOLATE, FAMISHED. THE SPARROWS were few, and anything that was to be had was good to eat.

On a bright morning in January, Mr. Morissot, a watch-maker by trade, but idler through circumstances, was walk-ing along the boulevard, sad, hungry, with his hands in the pockets of his uniform trousers, when he came face to face with a brother-in-arms whom he recognized as an old-time friend.

Before the war, Morissot could be seen at daybreak every Sunday, trudging along with a cane in one hand and a tin box on his back. He would take the train to Colombes and walk from there to the Isle of Marante where he would fish until dark.

It was there he had met Mr. Sauvage who kept a little notion store in the Rue Notre Dame de Lorette, a jovial fellow and passionately fond of fishing like himself. A warm friend-ship had sprung up between these two and they would fish side by side all day, very often without saying a word. Some days, when everything looked fresh and new and the beautiful spring sun gladdened every heart, Mr. Morissot would exclaim "How delightful!" and Mr. Sauvage would answer "There is nothing to equal it."

Then again on a fall evening, when the glorious setting sun, spreading its golden mantle on the already tinted leaves would throw strange shadows around the two friends, Sauvage would say "What a grand picture!"

"It beats the boulevard!" would answer Morissot. But they understood each other quite as well without speaking.

The two friends had greeted each other warmly and had resumed their walk side by side, both thinking deeply of the past and present events. They entered a *café*, and when a glass of absinthe had been placed before each Sauvage sighed.

"What terrible events, my friend!"

"And what weather!" said Morissot sadly; "this is the first nice day we have had this year. Do you remember our fishing excursions?"

"Do I! Alas! when shall we go again!"

After a second absinthe they emerged from the *café*, feeling rather dizzy—that light-headed effect which alcohol has on an empty stomach. The balmy air had made Sauvage exuberant and he exclaimed, "Suppose we go!"

"Where?"

"Fishing."

"Fishing! Where?"

"To our old spot, to Colombes. The French soldiers are

stationed near there and I know Colonel Dumoulin will give us a pass."

"It's a go; I am with you."

An hour after, having supplied themselves with their fishing tackle, they arrived at the colonel's villa. He had smiled at their request and had given them a pass in due form.

At about eleven o'clock they reached the advance-guard, and after presenting their pass, walked through Colombes and found themselves very near their destination. Argenteuil, across the way, and the great plains toward Nanterre were all deserted. Solitary the hill of Orgemont and Sannois rose clearly above the plains—a splendid point of observation.

"See," said Sauvage pointing to the hills. "The Prussians are there."

Prussians! They had never seen one, but they knew that they were all around Paris, invisible and powerful; plundering, devastating, and slaughtering. To their superstitious terror they added a deep hatred for this unknown and victorious people.

"What if we should meet some?" said Morissot.

"We would ask them to join us," said Sauvage in true Parisian style.

Still they hesitated to advance. The silence frightened them. Finally Sauvage picked up courage.

"Come, let us go on cautiously."

They proceeded slowly, hiding behind bushes, looking anxiously on every side, listening to every sound. A bare strip of land had to be crossed before reaching the river. They started to run. At last, they reached the bank and sank into the bushes, breathless but relieved.

Morissot thought he heard some one walking. He listened attentively, but no, he heard no sound. They were indeed alone! The little island shielded them from view. The house where the restaurant used to be seemed deserted; feeling reassured, they settled themselves for a good day's sport.

Sauvage caught the first fish, Morissot the second; and every minute they would bring one out which they would place in a net at their feet. It was indeed miraculous! They felt that supreme joy which one feels after having been deprived for months of a pleasant pastime. They had forgotten everything—even the war!

Suddenly, they heard a rumbling sound and the earth shook beneath them. It was the cannon on Mont Valérien. Morissot looked up and saw a trail of smoke, which was instantly followed by another explosion. Then they followed in quick succession.

"They are at it again," said Sauvage shrugging his shoulders. Morissot, who was naturally peaceful, felt a sudden, uncontrollable anger.

"Stupid fools! What pleasure can they find in killing each other!"

"They are worse than brutes!"

"It will always be thus as long as we have governments."

"Well, such is life!"

"You mean death!" said Morissot laughing.

They continued to discuss the different political problems, while the cannon on Mont Valérien sent death and desolation among the French.

Suddenly they started. They had heard a step behind them. They turned and beheld four big men in dark uniforms, with guns pointed right at them. Their fishing-lines dropped out of their hands and floated away with the current.

In a few minutes, the Prussian soldiers had bound them, cast them into a boat, and rowed across the river to the island which our friends had thought deserted. They soon found out their mistake when they reached the house, behind which stood a score or more of soldiers. A big burly officer, seated astride a chair, smoking an immense pipe, addressed them in excellent French. "Well, gentlemen, have you made a good haul?"

Just then, a soldier deposited at his feet the net full of fish which he had taken care to take along with him. The officer smiled and said: "I see you have done pretty well; but let us change the subject. You are evidently sent to spy upon me. You pretended to fish so as to put me off the scent, but I am not so simple. I have caught you and shall have you shot. I am sorry, but war is war. As you passed the advance-guard you certainly must have the password; give it to me, and I will set you free."

The two friends stood side by side, pale and slightly trembling, but they answered nothing.

"No one will ever know. You will go back home quietly and the secret will disappear with you. If you refuse, it is instant death! Choose!"

They remained motionless, silent. The Prussian officer calmly pointed to the river.

"In five minutes you will be at the bottom of this river! Surely, you have a family, friends waiting for you?"

Still they kept silent. The cannon rumbled incessantly. The officer gave orders in his own tongue, then moved his chair away from the prisoners. A squad of men advanced within twenty feet of them, ready for command.

"I give you one minute, not a second more!"

Suddenly approaching the two Frenchmen, he took Morissot aside and whispered: "Quick—the password. Your friend will not know; he will think I changed my mind." Morissot said nothing.

Then taking Sauvage aside he asked him the same thing, but he also was silent. The officer gave further orders and the men leveled their guns. At that moment, Morissot's eyes rested on the net full of fish lying in the grass a few feet away. The sight made him faint and, though he struggled against it, his eyes filled with tears. Then turning to his friend: "Farewell! Mr. Sauvage!"

"Farewell! Mr. Morissot."

They stood for a minute, hand in hand, trembling with emotion which they were unable to control.

"Fire!" commanded the officer.

The squad of men fired as one. Sauvage fell straight on his face. Morissot, who was taller, swayed, pivoted, and fell across his friend's body his face to the sky, while blood flowed freely from the wound in the breast. The officer gave further orders and his men disappeared. They came back presently with ropes and stones, which they tied to the feet of the two friends, and four of them carried them to the edge of the river. They swung them and threw them in as far as they could. The bodies weighted by stones sank immediately. A splash, a few ripples, and the water resumed its usual calmness. The only thing to be seen was a little blood floating on the surface. The officer calmly retraced his steps toward the house muttering. "The fish will get even now."

He perceived the net full of fish, picked it up, smiled, and called, "Wilhelm!"

A soldier in a white uniform approached. The officer handed him the fish saying: "Fry these little things while they are still alive; they will make a delicious meal."

And having resumed his position on the chair, he puffed away at his pipe.

The Culprit

Anton Chekhov

A PUNY LITTLE PEASANT, EXCEEDINGLY SKINNY, WEARING patched trousers and a shirt made of ticking, stands before the investigating magistrate. His hairy, pock-marked face, and his eyes, scarcely visible under thick, overhanging brows, have an expression of grim sullenness. The mop of tangled hair that has not known the touch of a comb for a long time gives him a spiderish air that makes him look even grimmer. He is barefoot.

"Denis Grigoryev!" the magistrate begins. "Step nearer and answer my questions. On the morning of the seventh of this present month of July, the railway watchman, Ivan Semyonovich Akinfov, making his rounds, found you, near the hundred-and-forty-first milepost, unscrewing the nut of one of the bolts by which the rails are fastened to the sleepers. Here is the nut! ... With the said nut he detained you. Is this true?"

"Wot?"

"Did all this happen as stated by Akinfov?"

"It did, sure."

"Very well; now, for what purpose were you unscrewing the nut?"

"Wot?"

"Stop saying 'wot' and answer the question: for what purpose were you unscrewing the nut?"

"If I didn't need it, I wouldn't've unscrewed it," croaks Denis, with a sidelong glance at the ceiling.

"What did you want that nut for?"

"The nut? We make sinkers of these nuts."

"Who are 'we'?"

"We, folks. . . . The Klimovo peasants, that is."

"Listen, brother; don't play the fool with me, but talk sense. There's no use lying to me about sinkers."

"I never lied in my life, and here I'm lying . . ." mutters Denis, blinking. "But can you do without a sinker, Your Honor? If you put live bait or worms on a hook, would it go to the bottom without a sinker? . . . So I'm lying," sneers Denis. "What the devil is the good of live bait if it floats on the surface? The perch and the pike and the eel-pout will bite only if your line touches bottom, and if your bait floats on the surface, it's only a bullhead will take it, and that only sometimes, and there ain't no bullhead in our river . . . That fish likes plenty of room."

"What are you telling me about bullhead for?"

"Wot? Why, you asked me yourself! Up our way the gentry catch fish that way, too. Even a little kid wouldn't try to catch fish without a sinker. No rules for fools."

"So you say you unscrewed this nut to make a sinker of it?"

"What else for? Not to play knucklebones with!"

"But you might have taken a bit of lead or a bullet for a sinker . . . a nail . . ."

"You don't pick up lead on the road, you have to pay for it, and a nail's no good. You can't find nothing better than a nut . . . It's heavy, and it's got a hole."

"He keeps playing the fool! As though he'd been born yesterday or dropped out of the sky! Don't you understand, you blockhead, what this unscrewing leads to? If the watchman hadn't been on the lookout, the train might have been derailed, people would have been killed—*you* would have killed people."

"God forbid, Your Honor! Kill people? Are we unbaptized, or criminals? Glory be to God, sir, we've lived our lives without dreaming of such a thing, much less killing anybody . . . Save us, Queen of Heaven, have mercy on us! What are you saying, sir?"

"And how do you suppose train wrecks happen? Unscrew two or three nuts, and you have a wreck!"

Denis sneers and screws up his eyes at the magistrate incredulously.

"Well! How many years have all of us here in the village been unscrewing nuts, and the Lord's protected us; and here you talk about wrecks, killing people. If I'd carried off a rail or put a log in the way, then maybe the train might've gone off the track, but . . . ppfff! a nut!"

"But try to get it into your head that the nut holds the rail fast to the sleepers!"

"We understand that . . . We don't unscrew all of 'em . . . We leave some . . . We don't do things without using our heads . . . We understand."

Denis yawns and makes the sign of the cross over his mouth.

"Last year a train was derailed here," says the magistrate. "Now it's plain why!"

"Beg pardon?"

"I say that it's plain why the train was derailed last year . . . Now I understand!"

"That's what you're educated for, our protectors, to understand. The Lord knew to whom to give understanding . . . Here you've figured out how and what, but the watchman, a peasant like us, with no brains at all, he gets you by the collar and pulls you in. You should figure it out first and then pull people in. But it's known, a peasant has the brains of a peasant. . . . Write down, too, Your Honor, that he hit me twice on the jaw, and on the chest, too."

"When your house was searched they found another nut. . . . At what spot did you unscrew that, and when?"

"You mean the nut under the little red chest?"

"I don't know where you kept it, but it was found. When did you unscrew it?"

"I didn't unscrew it; Ignashka, one-eyed Semyon's son, he gave it to me. I mean the one that was under the chest, but the one that was in the sledge in the yard, that one Mitrofan and I unscrewed together."

"Which Mitrofan?"

"Mitrofan Petrov . . . Didn't you hear of him? He makes nets and sells them to the gentry. He needs a lot of those nuts. Reckon a matter of ten for every net."

"Listen. According to Article 1081 of the Penal Code, deliberate damage to a railroad, calculated to jeopardize the trains, provided the perpetrator of the damage knew that it might cause an accident—you understand? Knew! And you couldn't help knowing what this unscrewing might lead to—is punishable by hard labor."

"Of course, you know best. . . We're ignorant folk. . . What do we understand?"

"You understand all about it! You are lying, faking!"

"Why should I lie? Ask in the village if you don't believe me. Only bleak is caught without a sinker. And a gudgeon's no kind of fish, but even gudgeon won't bite without a sinker."

"Tell me about bullhead, now," says the magistrate with a smile.

"There ain't no bullhead in our parts. . . . If we cast our lines without a sinker, with a butterfly for bait, we can maybe catch a chub that way, but even that not often."

"Now, be quiet."

There is silence. Denis shifts from one foot to the other, stares at the table covered with green cloth, and blinks violently as though he were looking not at cloth but at the sun. The magistrate writes rapidly.

"Can I go?" asks Denis, after a silence.

"No. I must put you in custody and send you to prison."

Denis stops blinking and, raising his thick eyebrows, looks inquiringly at the official.

"What do you mean, prison? Your Honor! I haven't the time; I must go to the fair; I must get three rubles from Yegor for lard!"

"Be quiet; don't disturb me."

"Prison . . . If I'd done something, I'd go; but to go just for nothing! What for? I didn't steal anything, so far as I know, I wasn't fighting . . . If there's any question about the arrears, Your Honor, don't believe the elder . . . Ask the permanent member of the Board . . . the elder, he's no Christian."

"Be quiet."

"I'm quiet as it is," mutters Denis; "as for the elder, he's lied about the assessment, I'll take my oath on it . . . We're three brothers: Kuzma Grigoryev, then Yegor Grigoryev, and me, Denis Grigoryev."

"You're disturbing me . . . Hey, Semyon," cries the magistrate, "take him out."

"We're three brothers," mutters Denis, as two husky soldiers seize him and lead him out of the chamber. "A brother don't have to answer for a brother. Kuzma don't pay, so you, Denis, have to answer for it . . . Judges! Our late master the general is dead—the Kingdom of Heaven be his!—or he'd have shown you judges what's what . . . You must have the know-how when you judge, not do it any which way . . . All right, flog a man, but justly, when it's coming to him."

A Wedding Gift

John Taintor Foote

GEORGE BALDWIN POTTER IS A PURIST. THAT IS TO SAY, HE either takes trout on a dry fly or he does not take them at all. He belongs to a number of fishing clubs, any member of which might acquire his neighbor's wife, beat his children, or poison a dog and still cast a fly, in all serenity, upon club waters; but should he impale on a hook a lowly though succulent worm and immerse the creature in those same waters it would be better that he send in his resignation at once, sooner than face the shaken committee that would presently wait upon him.

George had become fixed in my mind as a bachelor. This, of course, was a mistake. I am continually forgetting that purists rush into marriage when approaching or having just passed the age of forty. The psychology of this is clear.

For twenty years, let us say, a purist's life is completely filled by his efforts to convert all reasonable men to his own particular method of taking trout. He thinks, for example, that a man should not concern himself with more than a dozen types of standard flies. The manner of presenting them is the main consideration. Take any one of these flies, then, and place it, by means of an eight-foot rod, a light, tapered line, and a mist-colored leader of reasonable length, on fast water—if you want trout. Of course, if you want to listen to the birds and look at the scenery, fish the pools with a long line and an eight-foot leader. Why, it stands to reason that—

The years go by as he explains these vital facts patiently, again and again, to Smith and Brown and Jones. One wet, cold spring, after fighting a muddy stream all day, he reexplains for the better part of an evening and takes himself, somewhat wearily upstairs. The damp and chill of the room at whatever club he may be fishing is positively tomblike. He can hear the rain drumming on the roof and swishing against the windows. The water will be higher than ever tomorrow, he reflects, as he puts out the lights and slides between the icy sheets. Steeped to the soul in cheerless dark, he recalls numbly that when he first met Smith and Brown and Jones they were fishing the pools with a long line. That was, let's see—fifteen—eighteen—twenty years ago. Then he must be forty. It isn't possible! Yes, it is a fact that Smith and Brown and Jones are still fishing the pools with a long line.

In the first faint light of dawn he falls into an uneasy, muttering slumber. The dark hours between have been devoted to intense thought and a variety of wiggles which have not succeeded in keeping the bedclothes against his shoulder blades.

Some time within the next six months you will remember that you have forgotten to send him a wedding present.

George, therefore, having arrived at his fortieth birthday, announced his engagement shortly thereafter. Quite by chance I ran across his bride-to-be and himself a few days before the ceremony, and joined them at lunch. She was a blonde in the early twenties, with wide blue eyes and a typical rose-and-white complexion. A rushing, almost breathless account of herself, which she began the moment we were seated, was curious, I thought. It was as though she feared an interruption at any moment. I learned that she was an only child, born and reared in Greater New York; that her family had recently moved to New Rochelle; that she had been shopping madly for the past two weeks; that she was nearly dead, but that she had some adorable things.

At this point George informed me that they would spend their honeymoon at a certain fishing club in Maine. He then proceeded to describe the streams and lakes in that section at some length—during the rest of the luncheon, as a matter of fact. His fiancée, who had fallen into a wordless abstraction, only broke her silence with a vague murmur as we parted.

Owing to this meeting I did not forget to send a wedding present. I determined that my choice should please both George and his wife through the happy years to come.

If I had had George only to consider, I could have settled the business in two minutes at a sporting-goods store. Barred from these for obvious reasons, I spent a long day in a thoroughly exhausting search. Late in the afternoon I decided to abandon my hopeless task. I had made a tremendous effort and failed. I would simply buy a silver doodad and let it go at that.

As I staggered into a store with the above purpose in view, I passed a show case devoted to fine china, and halted as my eyes fell on a row of fish plates backed by artfully rumpled blue velvet. The plates proved to be hand painted. On each plate was one of the different varieties of trout, curving up through green depths to an artificial fly just dropping on the surface of the water.

In an automatic fashion I indicated the plates to a clerk, paid for them, gave him my card and the address, and fled from the store. Some time during the next twenty-four hours it came to me that George Potter was not among my nearest and dearest. Yet the unbelievable sum I had left with that clerk in exchange for those fish plates could be justified in no other way.

I thought this fact accounted for the sort of frenzy with which George flung himself upon me when next we met, some two months later. I had been week-ending in the country and encountered him in the Grand Central Station as I emerged from the lower level. For a long moment he wrung my hand in silence, gazing almost feverishly into my face. At last he spoke:

"Have you got an hour to spare?"

It occurred to me that it would take George an hour at least to describe his amazed delight at the splendor of my gift. The clock above Information showed that it was 12:45. I therefore suggested that we lunch together.

He, too, glanced at the clock, verified its correctness by his watch, and seized me by the arm.

"All right," he agreed, and was urging me toward the well-filled and somewhat noisy station café before I grasped his intention and tried to suggest that we go elsewhere. His hand only tightened on my arm.

"It's all right," he said; "good food, quick service—you'll like it."

He all but dragged me into the café and steered me to a table in the corner. I lifted my voice above an earnest clatter of gastronomical utensils and made a last effort.

"The Biltmore's just across the street."

George pressed me into my chair, shoved a menu card at me and addressed the waiter.

"Take his order." Here he jerked out his watch and consulted it again. "We have forty-eight minutes. Service for one. I shan't eat anything; or, no—bring me some coffee—large cup—black."

Having ordered mechanically, I frankly stared at George. He was dressed, I now observed, with unusual care. He wore a rather dashing gray suit. His tie, which was an exquisite shade of gray-blue, was embellished by a handsome pearl. The handkerchief, appearing above his breast pocket, was of the same delicate gray-blue shade as the tie. His face had been recently and closely shaven, also powdered; but above that smooth whiteness of jowl was a pair of curiously glittering eyes and a damp, a beaded brow. This he now mopped with his napkin.

"Good God," said I, "what is it, George?"

His reply was to extract a letter from his inside coat pocket and pass it across the table, his haunted eyes on mine. I took in its few lines at a glance:

Father has persuaded me to listen to what you call your explanation. I arrive Grand Central 2:45, daylight saving, Monday.

Isabelle

Poor old George, I thought; some bachelor indiscretion; and now, with his honeymoon scarcely over, blackmail, a lawsuit, heaven only knew what.

"Who," I asked, returning the letter, "is Isabelle?"

To my distress, George again resorted to his napkin. Then, "My wife," he said.

"Your wife!"

George nodded.

"Been living with her people for the last month. Wish he'd bring that coffee. You don't happen to have a flask with you?"

"Yes, I have a flask." George brightened. "But it's empty. Do you want to tell me about your trouble? Is that why you brought me here?"

"Well, yes," George admitted. "But the point is—will you stand by me? That's the main thing. She gets in"—here he consulted his watch—"in forty-five minutes, if the train's on time." A sudden panic seemed to seize him. His hand shot across the table and grasped my wrist. "You've got to stand by me, old man—until the ice is broken. That's all I ask. Just stick until the train gets in. Then act as if you knew nothing. Say you ran into me here and stayed to meet her. I'll tell you what—say I didn't seem to want you to stay. Kid me about wanting her all to myself, or something like that. Get the point? It'll give me a chance to sort of—well, you understand."

"I see what you mean, of course," I admitted. "Here's your coffee. Suppose you have some and then tell me what this is all about—if you care to, that is."

"No sugar, no cream," said George to the waiter; "just pour it. Don't stand there waving it about—pour it, pour it!" He attempted to swallow a mouthful of steaming coffee, gurgled frightfully and grabbed his water glass. "Great jumping Jehoshaphat!" he gasped, when he could speak, and glared at the waiter, who promptly moved out into the sea of diners and disappeared among a dozen of his kind.

"Steady, George," I advised as I transferred a small lump of ice from my glass to his coffee cup.

George watched the ice dissolve, murmured "Idiot" several times, and presently swallowed the contents of the cup in two gulps.

"I had told her," he said suddenly, "exactly where we were going. She mentioned Narragansett several times—I'll admit that. Imagine—Narragansett! Of course I bought her fishing things myself. I didn't buy knickers or woolens or flannel shirts—naturally. You don't go around buying a girl breeches and underwear before you're married. It wouldn't be—well, it isn't done, that's all. I got her the sweetest three-ounce rod you ever held in your hand. I'll bet I could put out sixty feet of line with it against the wind. I got her a pair of English waders that didn't weigh a pound. They cost me forty-five dollars. The rest of the outfit was just as good. Why, her fly box was a Truxton. I could have bought an American imitation for eight dollars. I know a lot of men who'll buy leaders for themselves at two dollars apiece and let their wives fish with any kind of tackle. I'll give you my word I'd have used anything I got for her myself. I sent it all out to be packed with her things. I wanted her to feel that it was her own—not mine. I know a lot of men who give their wives a high-class reel or an imported reel and then fish with it themselves. What time is it?"

"Clock right up there," I said. But George consulted his watch and used his napkin distressingly again.

"Where was I?"

"You were telling me why you sent her fishing things out to her."

"Oh, yes! That's all of that. I simply wanted to show you that from the first I did all any man could do. Ever been in the Cuddiwink district?"

I said that I had not.

"You go in from Buck's Landing. A lumber tug takes you up to the head of Lake Owonga. Club guides meet you there and put you through in one day—twenty miles by canoe and portage up the west branch of the Penobscot; then nine miles by trail to Lost Pond. The club's on Lost Pond. Separate cabins, with a main dining and loafing camp, and the best square-tail fishing on earth—both lake and stream. Of course, I don't fish the lakes. A dry fly belongs on a stream and nowhere else. Let me make it perfectly clear."

George's manner suddenly changed. He hunched himself closer to the table, dropped an elbow upon it and lifted an expository finger.

"The dry fly," he stated, with a new almost combative ring in his voice, "is designed primarily to simulate not only the appearance of the natural insect but its action as well. This action is arrived at through the flow of the current. The moment you move a fly by means of a leader you destroy the—

I saw that an interruption was imperative.

"Yes, of course," I said; but your wife will be here in—"

It was pitiful to observe George. His new-found assurance did not flee—flee suggests a withdrawal, however swift—it was immediately and totally annihilated. He attempted to pour himself some coffee, take out his watch, look at the clock, and mop his brow with his napkin at one and the same instant.

"You were telling me how to get to Lost Pond," I suggested.

"Yes, to be sure," said George. "Naturally you go in light. The things you absolutely have to have—rods, tackle, waders, wading shoes, and so forth, are about all a guide can manage at the portages in addition to the canoe. You pack in extras yourself—change of underclothes, a couple of pairs of socks, and a few toilet articles. You leave a bag or trunk at Buck's Landing.

I explained this to her. I explained it carefully. I told her either a week-end bag or one small trunk. Herb Trescott was my best man. I left everything to him. He saw us on the train and handed me tickets and reservations just before we pulled out. I didn't notice in the excitement of getting away that he'd given me three trunk checks all stamped 'Excess.' I didn't notice it till the conductor showed up, as a matter of fact. Then I said, 'Darling, what in heaven's name have you brought three trunks for?' She said—I can remember her exact words—'Then you're not going to Narragansett?'

"I simply looked at her. I was too dumbfounded to speak. At last I pulled myself together and told her in three days we'd be whipping the best squaretail water in the world. I took her hand, I remember, and said, 'You and I together, sweetheart,' or something like that."

George sighed and lapsed into a silence which remained unbroken until his eye happened to encounter the face of the clock. He started and went on:

"We got to Buck's Landing, by way of Bangor, at six in the evening of the following day. Buck's Landing is a railroad station with grass growing between the ties, a general store and hotel combined, and a lumber wharf. The store keeps canned peas, pink-and-white-candy, and felt boots. The hotel part is—well, it doesn't matter except that I don't think I ever saw so many deer heads; a few stuffed trout, but mostly deer heads. After supper the proprietor and I got the three trunks up to the largest room: We just got them in and that was all. The tug

left for the head of the lake at seven next morning. I explained
this to Isabelle. I said we'd leave the trunks there until we came
out, and offered to help her unpack the one her fishing things
were in. She said, 'Please go away!' So I went. I got out a rod
and went down to the wharf. No trout there, I knew; but I
thought I'd limber up my wrist. I put on a Cahill Number
Fourteen—or was it Sixteen—"

George knitted his brows and stared intently but unseeingly at me for some little time.

"Call it a Sixteen," I suggested.

George shook his head impatiently and remained concen-
trated in thought.

"I'm inclined to think it was a Fourteen," he said at last.
"But let it go; it'll come to me later. At any rate, the place was
alive with big chub—a foot long, some of 'em. I'll bet I took
fifty—threw 'em back, of course. They kept on rising after it
got dark. I'd tell myself I'd go after one more cast. Each time
I'd hook a big chub, and—well, you know how the time slips
away.

"When I got back to the hotel all the lights were out. I lit
matches until I got upstairs and found the door to the room.
I'll never forget what I saw when I opened that door—never!
Do you happen to know how many of the kind of things they
wear a woman can get into one trunk? Well, she had three
and she'd unpacked them all. She had used the bed for the
gowns alone. It was piled with them—literally piled; but that
wasn't a starter. Everywhere you looked was a stack of things

with ribbons in 'em. There were enough shoes and stockings for a girls' school; silk stockings, mind you, and high-heeled shoes and slippers." Here George consulted clock and watch. "I wonder if that train's on time," he wanted to know.

"You have thirty-five minutes, even if it is," I told him; "go right ahead."

"Well, I could see something was wrong from her face. I didn't know what, but I started right in to cheer her up. I told her all about the chub fishing I'd been having. At last she burst into tears. I won't go into the scene that followed. I'd ask her what was the matter and she'd say, 'Nothing,' and cry frightfully. I know a lot of men who would have lost their tempers under the circumstances, but I didn't; I give you my word. I simply said, 'There, there,' until she quieted down. And that isn't all. After a while she began to show me her gowns. Imagine—at eleven o'clock at night, at Buck's Landing! She'd hold up a dress and look over the top of it at me and ask me how I liked it, and I'd say it was all right. I know a lot of men who wouldn't have sat there two minutes.

"At last I said, 'They're all right, darling,' and yawned. She was holding up a pink dress covered with shiny dingle-dangles, and she threw the dress on the bed and all but had hysterics. It was terrible. In trying to think of some way to quiet her it occurred to me that I'd put her rod together and let her feel the balance of it with the reel I'd bought her—a genuine Fleetwood, mind you—attached. I looked around for her fishing things and couldn't find them. I'll tell you why I couldn't find them." George paused for an impressive instant to give his next words the full significance due them. "They weren't there!"

"No?" I murmured weakly.

"No," said George. "And what do you suppose she said when I questioned her? I can give you her exact words—I'll never forget them. She said, 'There wasn't any room for them.'" Again George paused. "I ask you," he inquired at last, "I ask you as man to man; what do you think of that?"

I found no adequate reply to this question and George, now thoroughly warmed up, rushed on.

"You'd swear I lost my temper then, wouldn't you? Well, I didn't. I did say something to her later, but I'll let you be the judge when we come to that. I'll ask you to consider the circumstances. I'll ask you to get Old Faithful in your mind's eye."

"Old Faithful?" I repeated. "Then you went to the Yellowstone later?"

"Yellowstone! Of course not! Haven't I told you we were already at the best trout water in America? Old Faithful was a squaretail. He'd been in the pool below Horseshoe Falls for twenty years, as a matter of record. We'll come to that presently. How are we off for time?"

"Thirty-one minutes," I told him. "I'm watching the clock—go ahead."

"Well, there she was, on a fishing trip with nothing to fish with. There was only one answer to that—she couldn't fish. But I went over everything she'd brought in three trunks and I'll give you my word she didn't have a garment of any sort you couldn't see through.

"Something had to be done and done quick, that was sure. I fitted her out from my own things with a sweater, a flannel shirt, and a pair of knickerbockers. Then I got the proprietor up and explained the situation. He got me some heavy underwear and two pairs of woolen stockings that belonged to his wife. When it came to shoes it looked hopeless, but the proprietor's wife, who had got up, too, by this time, thought of a pair of boy's moccasin's that were in the store and they turned out to be about the right size. I made arrangements to rent the room we had until we came out again to keep her stuff in, and took another room for the night—what was left of it after she'd repacked what could stay in the trunks and arranged what couldn't so it wouldn't be wrinkled.

"I got up early, dressed, and took my duffle down to the landing. I wakened her when I left the room. When breakfast was ready I went to see why she hadn't come down. She was all dressed, sitting on the edge of the bed. I said, 'Breakfast is ready, darling,' but I saw by her face that something was wrong again. It turned out to be my knickers. They fitted her perfectly—a little tight in spots—except in the waist. They would simply have fallen off if she hadn't held them up.

"Well, I was going in so light that I only had one belt. The proprietor didn't have any—he used suspenders. Neither did his wife—she used—well, whatever they use. He got me a piece of clothesline and I knotted it at each end and ran it through the what-you-may-call-'ems of the knickers and tied it in front. The knickers sort of puckered all the way round, but they couldn't come down—that was the main thing. I said, 'There you are, darling.' She walked over and tilted the mirror of the bureau so that she could see herself from head to foot. She said, 'Who are going to be at this place where we are going?' I said, 'Some of the very best dry-fly men in the country.' She said, 'I don't mean them; I mean the women. Will there be any women there?'

"I told her, certainly there would be women. I asked her if she thought I would take her into a camp with nothing but men. I named some of the women: Mrs. Fred Beal and Mrs. Brooks Carter and Talcott Ranning's sister and several more.

"She turned around slowly in front of the mirror, staring into it for a minute. Then she said, 'Please go out and close the door.' I said, 'All right, darling; but come right down. The tug will be here in fifteen minutes.'

"I went downstairs and waited ten minutes, then I heard the tug whistle for the landing and ran upstairs again. I knocked at the door. When she didn't answer I went in. Where do you suppose she was?"

I gave it up.

"In bed!" said George in an awe-struck voice. "In bed with her face turned to the wall; and listen, I didn't lose my temper as God is my judge. I rushed down to the wharf and told the tug captain I'd give him twenty-five dollars extra if he'd hold the boat till we came. He said all right and I went back to the room.

"The breeches had done it. She simply wouldn't wear them. I told her that at a fishing camp in Maine clothes were never thought of. I said, 'No one thinks of anything but trout, darling.' She said, 'I wouldn't let a fish see me looking like that.'" George's brow beaded suddenly. His hands dived searchingly into various pockets. "Got a cigarette? I left my case in my other suit."

He took a cigarette from me, lighted it with shaking fingers and inhaled deeply.

"It went on like that for thirty minutes. She was crying all the time, of course. I had started down to tell the tug captain it was all off, and I saw a woman's raincoat hanging in the hall. It belonged to some one up in one of the camps, the proprietor told me. I gave him seventy-five dollars to give to whoever owned it when he came out, and took it upstairs. In about ten minutes I persuaded her to wear it over the rest of her outfit until we got to camp. I told her one of the women would be able to fix her up all right when we got there. I didn't believe it, of course. The women at camp were all old-timers; they'd gone in as light as the men; but I had to say something.

"We had quite a trip going in. The guides were at the head of the lake all right—Indian Joe and a new man I'd never seen, called Charlie. I told Joe to take Isabelle—he's one of the best canoemen I ever saw. I was going to paddle bow for my man, but I'd have bet a cooky Indian Joe could stay with us on any kind of water. We had to beat it right through to make camp by night. It's a good stiff trip, but it can be done. I looked back at the other canoe now and then until we struck about a mile of white water that took all I had. When we were through the other canoe wasn't in sight. The river made a bend there, and I thought it was just behind and would show up any minute.

"Well, it didn't show up and I began to wonder. We hit our first portage about ten o'clock and landed. I watched downstream for twenty minutes, expecting to sight the other canoe every instant. Then Charlie, who hadn't opened his head, said, 'Better go back,' and put the canoe in again. We paddled downstream for all that was in it. I was stiff with fright. We saw 'em coming about three miles lower down and back-paddled till they came up. Isabelle was more cheerful-looking than she'd been since we left New York, but Joe had that stony face an Indian gets when he's sore.

"I said, 'Anything wrong?' Joe just grunted and drove the canoe past us. Then I saw it was filled with wild flowers. Isabelle said she'd been picking them right off the banks all the way long. She said she'd only had to get out of the boat once, for the blue ones. Now, you can't beat that—not in a thousand years. I leave it to you if you can. Twenty miles of stiff current, with five portages ahead of us and a nine-mile hike at the end of that. I gave that Indian the devil for letting her do such a thing, and tipped the flowers into the Penobscot when we unloaded for the first portage. She didn't speak to me on the portage, and she got into her canoe without a word.

"Nothing more happened going in, except this flower business had lost us two hours, and it was so dark when we struck the swamp at Loon Lake that we couldn't follow the trail well and kept stumbling over down timber and stepping into bog holes. She was about fagged out by then, and the mosquitoes were pretty thick through there. Without any warning she sat down in the trail. She did it so suddenly I nearly fell over her. I asked her what was the matter and she said, 'This is the end'—just like that—'this is the end!' I said, 'The end of what, darling. Just think, to-morrow we'll be on the best trout water in the world!' With that she said, 'I want my mother, my darling mother,' and bowed her head in her hands. Think it over, please; and remember, I didn't lose my temper. You're sure there's nothing left in your flask?"

"Not a drop, George," I assured him. "Go ahead; we've only twenty-five minutes."

George looked wildly at the clock, then at his watch.

"A man never has it when he wants it most. Have you noticed that? Where was I?"

"You were in the swamp."

"Oh, yes! Well, she didn't speak after that, and nothing I could say would budge her. The mosquitoes had got wind of us when we stopped and were coming in swarms. We'd be eaten alive in another ten minutes. So I told Joe to give his pack to Charlie and help me pick her up and carry her. Joe said, 'No, by damn!' and folded his arms. When an Indian gets sore he stays sore, and when he's sore he's stubborn. The mosquitoes were working on him good and plenty, though, and at last he said, 'Me carry packs. Charlie help carry—that.' He flipped his hand over in the direction of Isabelle and took the pack from Charlie.

"It was black as your hat by now, and the trail through there was only about a foot wide with swamp on each side. It was going to be some job getting her out of there. I thought Charlie and I would make a chair of our arms and stumble along with her some way; but when I started to lift her up she said, 'Don't touch me!' and got up and went on. A blessing if there ever was one. We got to camp at ten that night.

"She was stiff and sore next morning—you expect it after a trip like that—besides, she'd caught a little cold. I asked her how she felt, and she said she was going to die and asked me to send for a doctor and her mother. The nearest doctor was at Bangor and her mother was in New Rochelle. I carried her breakfast over from the dining camp to our cabin. She said she couldn't eat any breakfast, but she did drink a cup of coffee, telling me between sips how awful it was to die alone in a place like that.

"After she'd had the coffee she seemed to feel better. I went to the camp library and got *The Dry Fly on American Waters*, by Charles Darty. I consider him the soundest man in the country. He's better than Pell or Fawcett. My chief criticism of him is that in his chapter on Streams East of the Alleghenies— east of the Alleghenies, mind you—he recommends the Royal Coachman. I consider the Lead-Wing Coachman a serviceable fly on clear, hard-fished water; but the Royal—never! I wouldn't give it a shade over the Professor or the Montreal.

Just consider the body alone of the Royal Coachman—never mind the wings and hackle—the body of the Royal is—"

"Yes, I know, George," I said; "but—"

I glanced significantly at the clock. George started, sighed, and resumed his narrative.

"I went back to the cabin and said, 'Darling, here is one of the most intensely interesting books ever written. I'm going to read it aloud to you. I think I can finish it to-day. Would you like to sit up in bed while I read?' She said she hadn't strength enough to sit up in bed, so I sat down beside her and started reading. I had read about an hour, I suppose, when she did sit up in bed quite suddenly. I saw she was staring at me in a queer, wild way that was really startling. I said, 'What is it, darling?' She said, 'I'm going to get up. I'm going to get up this instant.'

"Well, I was delighted, naturally. I thought the book would get her by the time I'd read it through. But there she was, as keen as mustard before I'd got well into it. I'll tell you what I made up my mind to do, right there. I made up my mind to let her use my rod that day. Yes, sir—my three-ounce Spinoza, and what's more, I did it."

George looked at me triumphantly, then lapsed into reflection for a moment.

"If ever a man did everything possible to—well, let it go. The main thing is, I have nothing to reproach myself with—nothing. Except—but we'll come to that presently. Of course, she wasn't ready for dry flies yet. I borrowed some wet flies from the club steward, got some cushions for the canoe and put my rod together. She had no waders, so a stream was out of the question. The lake was better, anyway, that first day; she'd have all the room she wanted for her back cast.

"I stood on the landing with her before we got into the canoe and showed her just how to put out a fly and recover it. Then she tried it." A sort of horror came into George's face. "You wouldn't believe any one could handle a rod like that," he said huskily. "You couldn't believe it unless you'd seen it. Gimme a cigarette.

"I worked with her a half hour or so and saw no improvement—none whatever. At last she said, 'The string is too long. I can't do anything with such a long string on the pole.' I told her gently—gently, mind you—that the string was an eighteen-dollar double-tapered Hurdman line, attached to a Gebhardt reel on a three-ounce Spinoza rod. I said, 'We'll go out on the lake now. If you can manage to get a rise, perhaps it will come to you instinctively.'

"I paddled her out on the lake and she went at it. She'd spat the flies down and yank them up and spat them down again. She hooked me several times with her back cast and got tangled up in the line herself again and again. All this time I was speaking quietly to her, telling her what to do. I give you my word I never raised my voice—not once—and I thought she'd break the tip every moment.

"Finally she said her arm was tired and lowered the rod. She'd got everything messed up with her last cast and the flies were trailing just over the side of the canoe. I said, 'Recover your cast and reel in, darling.' Instead of using her rod, she took hold of the leader close to the flies and started to pull them into the canoe. At that instant a little trout—couldn't have been over six inches—took the tail fly. I don't know exactly what happened, it was all over so quickly. I think she just screamed and let go of everything. At any rate, I saw my Spinoza bounce off the gunwale of the canoe and disappear. There was fifty feet of water just there. And now listen carefully: not one word did I utter—not one. I simply turned the canoe and paddled to the landing in absolute silence. No reproaches of any sort. Think that over!"

I did. My thoughts left me speechless. George proceeded:

"I took out a guide and tried dragging for the rod with a gang hook and heavy sinker all the rest of the day. But the gangs would only foul on the bottom. I gave up at dusk and paddled in. I said to the guide—it was Charlie—I said, 'Well, it's all over, Charlie.' Charlie said, 'I brought Mr. Carter in and he had an extra rod. Maybe you could borrow it. It's a four-ounce Meecham.' I smiled. I actually smiled. I turned and looked at the lake. 'Charlie,' I said, 'somewhere out there in that dark water, where the eye of man will never behold it again, is a three-ounce Spinoza—and you speak of a Meecham.' Charlie said, 'Well, I just thought I'd tell you.' I said, 'That's all right, Charlie. That's all right.' I went to the main camp, saw Jean, the head guide and made arrangements to leave the next day. Then I went to our cabin and sat down before the fire. I heard

Isabelle say something about being sorry. I said, 'I'd rather not talk about it, darling. If you don't mind, we'll never mention it again.' We sat there in silence, then, until dinner.

"As we got up from dinner, Nate Griswold and his wife asked us to play bridge with them that evening. I'd told no one what had happened, and Nate didn't know, of course. I simply thanked him and said we were tired, and we went back to our cabin. I sat down before the fire again. Isabelle seemed restless. At last she said, 'George.' I said, 'What is it, darling?' She said, 'Would you like to read to me from that book?' I said, 'I'm sorry, darling; if you don't mind I'll just sit here quietly by the fire.'

"Somebody knocked at the door after a while. I said, 'Come in.' It was Charlie. I said, 'What is it, Charlie?' Then he told me that Bob Frazer had been called back to New York and was going out next morning. I said, 'Well, what of it?' Charlie said, 'I just thought you could maybe borrow his rod.' I said, 'I thought you understood about that, Charlie.' Charlie said, 'Well, that's it. Mr. Frazer's rod is a three-ounce Spinoza.'

"I got up and shook hands with Charlie and gave him five dollars. But when he'd gone I began to realize what was before me. I'd brought in a pint flask of prewar Scotch. Prewar—get that! I put this in my pocket and went over to Bob's cabin. Just as I was going to knock I lost my nerve. I sneaked away from the door and went down to the lake and sat on the steps of the canoe landing. I sat there for quite a while and took several nips. At last I thought I'd just go and tell Bob of my loss and see what he said. I went back to his cabin and this time I knocked. Bob was putting a few odds and ends in a shoulder pack. His rod was in its case, standing against the wall.

"I said, 'I hear you're going out in the morning.' He said, 'Yes, curse it, my wife's mother has to have some sort of a damned operation or other.' I said, 'How would a little drink strike you, Bob?' He said, 'Strike me! Wait a minute! What kind of a drink?' I took out the flask and handed it to him. He unscrewed the cap and held the flask to his nose. He said, 'Great heavens above, it smells like—' I said, 'It is.' He said, 'It can't be!' I said, 'Yes, it is.' He said, 'There's a trick in it somewhere.' I said, 'No, there isn't—I give you my word.' He tasted what was in the flask carefully. Then he said, 'I call this white of you, George,' and took a good stiff snort. When he was handing back the flask he said, 'I'll do as much for you some day, if I ever get the chance.' I took a snifter myself.

"Then I said, 'Bob, something awful has happened to me. I came here to tell you about it.' He said, 'Is that so? Sit down.' I sat down and told him. He said, 'What kind of a rod was it?' I said, 'A three-ounce Spinoza.' He came over and gripped my hand without a word. I said, 'Of course, I can't use anything else.' He nodded, and I saw his eyes flicker toward the corner of the room where his own rod was standing. I said, 'Have another drink, Bob.' But he just sat down and stared at me. I took a good stiff drink myself. Then I said, 'Under ordinary circumstances, nothing on earth could hire me to ask a man to—' I stopped right there.

"Bob got up suddenly and began to walk up and down the room. I said, 'Bob, I'm not considering myself—not for a minute. If it was last season, I'd simply have gone back tomorrow without a word. But I'm not alone any more. I've got the little girl to consider. She's never seen a trout taken in her life—think of it, Bob! And here she is, on her honeymoon, at the best water I know of. On her honeymoon, Bob!' I waited for him to say something, but he went to the window and stared out, with his back to me. I got up and said good-night and started for the door. Just as I reached it he turned from the window and rushed over and picked up his rod. He said, 'Here, take it,' and put the rod case in my hands. I started to try to thank him, but he said, 'Just go ahead with it,' and pushed me out the door."

The waiter was suddenly hovering above us with his eyes on the dishes.

"Now what do you want?" said George.

"Never mind clearing here," I said. "Just bring me the check. Go ahead, George."

"Well, of course, I can't any more than skim what happened finally, but you'll understand. It turned out that Ernie Payton's wife had an extra pair of knickers and she loaned them to Isabelle. I was waiting outside the cabin while she dressed next morning, and she called out to me. 'Oh, George, they fit!' Then I heard her begin to sing. She was a different girl when she came out to go to breakfast. She was almost smiling. She'd done nothing but slink about the day before. Isn't it extraordinary what will seem important to a woman? Gimme a cigarette."

"Fifteen minutes, George," I said as I supplied him.

"Yes, yes, I know. I fished the Cuddiwink that day. Grand stream, grand. I used a Pink Lady—first day on a stream with Isabelle—little touch of sentiment—and it's a darn good fly. I fished it steadily all day. Or did I try a Seth Green about noon? It seems to me I did, now that I recall it. It seems to me that where the Katahdin brook comes in I—"

"It doesn't really matter, does it, George?" I ventured.

"Of course, it matters!" said George decisively. "A man wants to be exact about such things. The precise details of what happens in a day's work on a stream are of real value to yourself and others. Except in the case of a record fish, it isn't important that you took a trout; it's exactly how you took him that's important."

"But the time, George," I protested.

He glanced at the clock, swore softly, mopped his brow—this time with the blue-gray handkerchief—and proceeded.

"Isabelle couldn't get into the stream without waders, so I told her to work along the bank a little behind me. It was pretty thick along there, second growth and vines mostly; but I was putting that Pink Lady on every foot of good water and she kept up with me easily enough. She didn't see me take many trout, though. I'd look for her, after landing one, to see what she thought of the way I'd handled the fish, and almost invariably she was picking ferns or blueberries, or getting herself untangled from something. Curious things, women. Like children, when you stop to think of it."

George stared at me unseeingly for a moment.

"And you never heard of Old Faithful?" he asked suddenly. "Evidently not, from what you said a while ago. Well, a lot of people have, believe me. Men have gone to the Cuddiwink district just to see him. As I've already told you, he lay beside a ledge in the pool below Horseshoe Falls. Almost nothing else in the pool. He kept it cleaned out. Worst sort of cannibal, of course—all big trout are. That was the trouble—he wanted something that would stick to his ribs. No flies for him. Did his feeding at night.

"You could see him dimly if you crawled out on a rock that jutted above the pool and looked over. He lay in about ten feet of water, right by his ledge. If he saw you he'd back under the ledge, slowly, like a submarine going into dock. Think of the biggest thing you've ever seen, and that's the way Old Faithful looked, just lying there as still as the ledge. He never seemed to move anything, not even his gills. When he backed in out of sight he seemed to be drawn under the ledge by some invisible force.

"Ridgway—R. Campbell Ridgway—you may have read his stuff, Brethren of the Wild, that sort of thing—claimed to have seen him move. He told me about it one night. He said he was lying with just his eyes over the edge of the rock, watching the trout. Said he'd been there an hour, when down over the falls came a young red squirrel. It had fallen in above and been carried over. The squirrel was half drowned, but struck out feebly for shore. Well, so Ridgway said—Old Faithful came up and took Mister Squirrel into camp. No hurry; just came drifting up, sort of inhaled the squirrel and sank down to the ledge again. Never made a ripple. Ridgway said; just business.

"I'm telling you all this because it's necessary that you get an idea of that trout in your mind. You'll see why in a minute. No one ever had hold of him. But it was customary, if you fished the Cuddiwink, to make a few casts over him before you left the stream. Not that you ever expected him to rise. It was just a sort of gesture. Everybody did it.

"Knowing that Isabelle had never seen trout taken before, I made a day of it—naturally. The trail to camp leaves the stream just at the falls. It was pretty late when we got to it. Isabelle had her arms full of—heaven knows what—flowers and grass and ferns and fir branches and colored leaves. She'd lugged the stuff for hours. I remember once that day I was fighting a fourteen-inch fish in swift water and she came to the bank and wanted me to look at a ripe blackberry—I think it was—she'd found. How does that strike you? And listen! I said, 'It's a beauty, darling.' That's what I said—or something like that. . . . Here, don't you pay that check! Bring it here, waiter!"

"Go on, George!" I said. "We haven't time to argue about the check. You'd come to the trail for camp at the falls."

"I told Isabelle to wait at the trail for a few minutes, while I went below the falls and did the customary thing for the edification of Old Faithful. I only intended to make three or four casts with the Number Twelve Fly and the hair-fine leader I had on, but in getting down to the pool I hooked the fly in a bush. In trying to loosen it I stumbled over something and fell. I snapped the leader like a thread, and since I had to put on another, I tied on a fairly heavy one as a matter of form.

"I had reached for my box for a regulation fly of some sort when I remembered a fool thing that Billy Roach had given me up on the Beaverkill the season before. It was fully two inches long; I forget what he called it. He said you fished it dry for bass or large trout. He said you worked the tip of your rod and made it wiggle like a dying minnow. I didn't want the contraption, but he'd borrowed some fly oil from me and insisted on my taking it. I'd stuck it in the breast pocket of my fishing jacket and forgotten it until then.

"Well, I felt in the pocket and there it was. I tied it on and went down to the pool. Now let me show you the exact situation." George seized a fork. "This is the pool." The fork traced an oblong figure on the tablecloth. "Here is Old Faithful's ledge." The fork deeply marked this impressive spot. "Here are the falls, with white water running to here. You can only wade to this point here, and then you have an abrupt six-foot depth. 'But you can put a fly from here to here with a long line,' you say. No, you can't. You've forgotten to allow for your back cast. Notice this bend here? That tells the story. You're not more than twenty feet from a lot of birch and whatnot, when you can no longer wade. 'Well, then, it's impossible to put a decent fly on the water above the sunken ledge,' you say. It looks like it, but this is how it's done: right here is a narrow point run-ning to here, where it dwindles off to a single flat rock. If you work out on the point you can jump across to this rock—situated right there—and there you are, with about a thirty-foot cast to the sunken ledge. Deep water all around you, of course, and the rock is slippery; but—there you are. Now notice this small cove, right there. The water from the falls rushes past it in a froth, but in the cove it forms a deep eddy, with the cur-rent moving round and round, like this." George made a slow circular motion with the fork. "You know what I mean?"

I nodded.

"I got out on the point and jumped to the rock; got myself balanced, worked out the right amount of line and cast the dingaree Bill had forced on me, just above the sunken ledge. I didn't take the water lightly and I cast again, but I couldn't put it down decently. It would just flop in—too much weight and too many feathers. I suppose I cast it a dozen times, trying to make it settle like a fly. I wasn't thinking of trout—there would be nothing in there except Old Faithful—I was just monkey-ing with this doodle-bug thing, now that I had it on.

"I gave up at last and let it lie out where I had cast it. I was standing there looking at the falls roaring down, when I remembered Isabelle, waiting up on the trail. I raised my rod preparatory to reeling in and the what-you-may-call-'em made a kind of a dive and wiggle out there on the surface. I reached for my reel handle. Then I realized that the thingamajig wasn't on the water. I didn't see it disappear, exactly; I was just looking at it, and then it wasn't there. 'That's funny,' I thought, and struck instinctively. Well, I was fast—so it seemed—and no snags in there. I gave it the butt three or four times, but the rod only bowed and nothing budged. I tried to figure it out. I thought perhaps a water-logged timber had come diving over the falls and upended right there. Then I noticed the rod take more of a bend and the line began to move through the water. It moved out slowly, very slowly, into the middle of the pool. It was exactly as though I was hooked on to a freight train just getting under way.

"I knew what I had hold of then, and yet I didn't believe it. I couldn't believe it. I kept thinking it was a dream. I remember. Of course, he could have gone away with everything I had any minute if he'd wanted to, but he didn't. He just kept moving slowly, round and round the pool. I gave him what pressure the tackle would stand, but he never noticed a little thing like that; just kept moving around the pool for hours, it seemed to me. I'd forgotten Isabelle; I admit that. I'd forgotten everything on earth. There didn't seem to be anything else on earth, as a matter of fact, except the falls and the pool and Old Faithful and me. At last Isabelle showed up on the bank above me, still lugging her ferns and whatnot. She called down to me above the noise of the falls. She asked me how long I expected her to wait alone in the woods, with night coming on.

"I hadn't had the faintest idea how I was going to try to land the fish until then. The water was boiling past the rock I was standing on, and I couldn't jump back to the point without giving him slack and perhaps falling in. I began to look around and figure. Isabelle, said, 'What on earth are you doing?' I took off my landing net and tossed it to the bank. I yelled, 'Drop that junk quick and pick up that net!' She said, 'What for, George?' I said, 'Do as I tell you and don't ask questions!' She laid down what she had and picked up the net and I told her to go to the cove and stand ready.

"She said, 'Ready for what?' I said, 'You'll see what presently. Just stand there.' I'll admit I wasn't talking quietly. There was the noise of the falls to begin with, and—well, naturally I wasn't.

"I went to work on the fish again. I began to educate him to lead. I thought if I could lead him into the cove he would swing right past Isabelle and she could net him. It was slow work—a three-ounce rod—imagine! Isabelle called, 'Do you know what time it is?' I told her to keep still and stand where she was. She didn't say anything more after that.

"At last the fish began to come. He wasn't tired—he'd never done any fighting, as a matter of fact—but he'd take a suggestion as to where to go from the rod. I kept swinging him nearer and nearer the cove each time he came around. When I saw he was about ready to come I yelled to Isabelle. I said, 'I'm going to bring him right past you, close to the top. All you have to do is to net him.'

"When the fish came round again I steered him into the cove. Just as he was swinging past Isabelle the stuff she'd been lugging began to roll down the bank. She dropped the landing net on top of the fish and made a dive for those leaves and grasses and things. Fortunately the net handle lodged against the bank, and after she'd put her stuff in a nice safe place she came back and picked up the net again. I never uttered a syllable. I deserve no credit for that. The trout had made a surge and shot out into the pool and I was too busy just then to give her any idea of what I thought.

"I had a harder job getting him to swing in again. He was a little leery of the cove, but at last he came. I steered him toward Isabelle and lifted him all I dared. He came up nicely, clear to the top. I yelled, 'Here he comes! For God's sake, don't miss him!' I put everything on the tackle it would stand and managed to check the fish for an instant right in front of Isabelle.

"And this is what she did: it doesn't seem credible—it doesn't seem humanly possible; but it's a fact that you'll have to take my word for. She lifted the landing net above her head with both hands and brought it down on top of the fish with all her might!"

George ceased speaking. Despite its coating of talcum powder, I was able to detect an additional pallor in his countenance.

"Will I ever forget it as long as I live?" he inquired at last.

"No, George," I said, "but we've just exactly eleven minutes left."

George made a noticeable effort and went on:

"By some miracle the fish stayed on the hook; but I got a faint idea of what would have happened if he'd taken a real notion to fight. He went around the pool so fast it must have made him dizzy. I heard Isabelle say, 'I didn't miss him, George'; and then—well, I didn't lose my temper; you wouldn't call it that exactly. I hardly knew what I said. I'll admit I shouldn't have said it. But I did say it; no doubt of that; no doubt of that whatever."

"What was it you said?" I asked.

George looked at me uneasily.

"Oh, the sort of thing a man would say impulsively—under the circumstances."

"Was it something disparaging about her?" I inquired.

"Oh, no," said George, "nothing about her. I simply intimated—in a somewhat brutal way, I suppose—that she'd better get away from the pool—er—not bother me any more is what I meant to imply."

For the first time since George had chosen me for a confidant I felt a lack of frankness on his part.

"Just what did you say, George?" I insisted.

"Well, it wasn't altogether my words," he evaded. "It was the tone I used, as much as anything. Of course, the circumstances would excuse—Still, I regret it. I admit that. I've told you so plainly."

There was no time in which to press him further.

"Well, what happened then?" I asked.

"Isabelle just disappeared. She went up the bank, of course, but I didn't see her go. Old Faithful was still nervous and I had to keep my eye on the line. He quieted down in a little while and continued to promenade slowly around the pool. I suppose this kept up for half an hour more. Then I made up my mind that something had to be done. I turned very carefully on the rock, lowered the tip until it was on a line with the fish, turned the rod under my arm until it was pointing behind me and jumped.

"Of course, I had to give him slack; but I kept my balance on the point by the skin of my teeth, and when I raised the rod he was still on. I worked to the bank, giving out line, and crawled under some bushes and things and got around to the cove at last. Then I started to work again to swing him into the cove, but absolutely nothing doing. I could lead him anywhere except into the cove. He'd had enough of that; I didn't blame him, either.

"To make a long story short, I stayed with him for two hours. For a while it was pretty dark; but there was a good-sized moon that night, and when it rose it shone right down on the pool through a gap in the trees fortunately. My wrist was gone completely, but I managed to keep some pressure on him all the time, and at last he forgot about what had happened to him in the cove. I swung him in and the current brought him past me. He was on his side by now. I don't think he was tired even then—just discouraged. I let him drift over the net, heaved him out on the bank and sank down beside him, absolutely all in. I couldn't have got to my feet on a bet. I just sat there in a sort of daze and looked at Old Faithful, gleaming in the moonlight.

"After a half-hour's rest I was able to get up and go to camp. I planned what I was going to do on the way. There was always a crowd in the main camp living room after dinner. I simply walked into the living room without a word and laid Old Faithful on the center table.

"Well, you can imagine faintly what happened. I never got any dinner—couldn't have eaten any, as a matter of fact. I didn't even get a chance to take off my waders. By the time I'd told just how I'd done it to one crowd, more would come in and look at Old Faithful; and then stand and look at me for a while; and then make me tell it all over again. At last everybody began to dig up anything they had with a kick in it. Almost every one had a bottle he'd been hoarding. There was Scotch and gin and brandy and rye and a lot of experimental stuff. Art Bascom got a tin dish pan from the kitchen and put it on the table beside Old Faithful. He said, 'Pour your contributions right in here, men.' So each man dumped whatever he had into the dish pan and everybody helped himself.

"It was great, of course. The biggest night of my life, but I hope I'll never be so dog-tired again. I felt as though I'd taken a beating. After they'd weighed Old Faithful—nine pounds five and a half ounces; and he'd been out of water two hours—I said I had to go to bed, and went.

"Isabelle wasn't in the cabin. I thought, in a hazy way, that she was with some of the women, somewhere. Don't get the idea I was stewed. But I hadn't had anything to eat, and the mixture in that dish pan was plain TNT.

"I fell asleep as soon as I hit the bed; slept like a log till daylight. Then I half woke up, feeling that something terrific had happened. For a minute I didn't know what; then I remembered what it was. I had landed Old Faithful on a three-ounce rod!

"I lay there and went over the whole thing from the beginning, until I came to Isabelle with the landing net. That made me look at where her head should have been on the pillow. It wasn't there. She wasn't in the cabin. I thought perhaps she'd got up early and gone out to look at the lake or the sunrise or something. But I got up in a hurry and dressed.

"Well, I could see no signs of Isabelle about camp. I ran into Jean just coming from the head guide's cabin and he said, 'Too bad about your wife's mother.' I said, 'What's that?' He repeated what he'd said, and added, 'She must be an awful sick woman.' Well, I got out of him finally that Isabelle had come straight up from the stream the evening before, taken two guides and started for Buck's Landing. Jean had urged her to wait until morning, naturally; but she'd told him she must get to her mother at once, and took on so, as Jean put it, that he had to let her go.

"I said, 'Let me have Indian Joe, stern, and a good man, bow. Have 'em ready in ten minutes.' I rushed to the kitchen, drank two cups of coffee and started for Buck's Landing. We made the trip down in seven hours, but Isabelle had left with her trunks on the 10:40 train.

"I haven't seen her since. Went to her home once. She wouldn't see me; neither would her mother. Her father advised not forcing things—just waiting. He said he'd do what he could. Well, he's done it—you read the letter. Now you know the whole business. You'll stick, of course, and see me through just the first of it, old man. Of course, you'll do that, won't you? We'd better get down to the train now. Track Nineteen."

George rose from the table. I followed him from the café, across the blue-domed rotunda to a restraining rope stretched before the gloomy entrance to Track Nineteen.

"George," I said, "one thing more: just what did you say to her when she—"

"Oh, I don't know," George began vaguely.

"George," I interrupted, "no more beating about the bush. What did you say?"

I saw his face grow even more haggard, if possible. Then it mottled into a shade resembling the brick on an old colonial mansion.

"I told her—" he began in a low voice.

"Yes?" I encouraged.

"I told her to get the hell out of there."

And now a vision was presented to my mind's eye; a vision of twelve fish plates, each depicting a trout curving up through green waters to an artificial fly. The vision extended on through the years. I saw Mrs. George Baldwin Potter ever gazing upon those rising trout and recalling the name on the card which had accompanied them to her door.

I turned and made rapidly for the main entrance of the Grand Central Station. In doing so I passed the clock above

Information and saw that I still had two minutes in which to be conveyed by a taxicab far, far from the entrance to Track Nineteen.

I remember hearing the word "quitter" hurled after me by a hoarse, despairing voice.

A Fatal Success

Henry van Dyke

BEEKMAN DE PEYSTER WAS PROBABLY THE MOST PASSIONATE
and triumphant fisherman in the Petrine Club. He angled with
the same dash and confidence that he threw into his opera-
tions in the stock-market. He was sure to be the first man to
get his flies on the water at the opening of the season. And
when we came together for our fall meeting, to compare notes
of our wanderings on various streams and make up the fish-
stories for the year, Beekman was almost always "high hook."
We expected, as a matter of course, to hear that he had taken
the most and the largest fish.

It was so with everything that he undertook. He was a
masterful man. If there was an unusually large trout in a river,
Beekman knew about it before any one else, and got there first,
and came home with the fish. It did not make him unduly
proud, because there was nothing uncommon about it. It was
his habit to succeed, and all the rest of us were hardened to it.

When he married Cornelia Cochrane, we were consoled
for our partial loss by the apparent fitness and brilliancy of
the match. If Beekman was a masterful man, Cornelia was

certainly what you might call a mistressful woman. She had been the head of her house since she was eighteen years old. She carried her good looks like the family plate; and when she came into the breakfast-room and said good-morning, it was with an air as if she presented every one with a check for a thousand dollars. Her tastes were accepted as judgments, and her preferences had the force of laws. Wherever she wanted to go in the summertime, there the finger of household destiny pointed. At Newport, at Bar Harbor, at Lenox, at Southampton, she made a record. When she was joined in holy wedlock to Beekman De Peyster, her father and mother heaved a sigh of satisfaction, and settled down for a quiet vacation in Cherry Valley.

It was in the second summer after the wedding that Beekman admitted to a few of his ancient Petrine cronies, in moments of confidence (unjustifiable, but natural), that his wife had one fault.

"It is not exactly a fault," he said, "not a positive fault, you know. It is just a kind of a defect, due to her education, of course. In everything else she's magnificent. But she doesn't care for fishing. She says it's stupid—can't see why any one should like the woods—calling camping out the lunatic's diversion. It's rather awkward for a man with my habits to have his wife take such a view. But it can be changed by training. I intend to educate her and convert her. I shall make an angler of her yet."

And so he did.

The new education was begun in the Adirondacks, and the first lesson was given at Paul Smith's. It was a complete failure.

Beekman persuaded her to come out with him for a day on Meacham River, and promised to convince her of the charm of angling. She wore a new gown, fawn-colour and violet, with a picture-hat, very taking. But the Meacham River trout was shy that day; not even Beekman could induce him to rise to the fly. What the trout lacked in confidence the mosquitoes more than made up. Mrs. De Peyster came home much sunburned, and expressed a highly unfavorable opinion of fishing as an amusement and of Meacham River as a resort.

"The nice people don't come to the Adirondacks to fish," said she; "they come to talk about the fishing twenty years ago. Besides, what do you want to catch that trout for? If you do, the other men will say you bought it, and the hotel will have to put in another for the rest of the season."

The following year Beekman tried Moosehead Lake. Here he found an atmosphere more favourable to his plan of education. There were a good many people who really fished, and short expeditions in the woods were quite fashionable. Cornelia had a camping-costume of the most approved style made by Dewlap on Fifth Avenue—pearl-gray with linings of rose-silk—and consented to go with her husband on a trip up Moose River. They pitched their tent the first evening at the mouth of Misery Stream, and a storm came on. The rain sifted through the canvas in a fine spray, and Mrs. De Peyster sat up all night in a waterproof cloak, holding an umbrella. The next day they were back at the hotel in time for lunch.

"It was horrid," she told her most intimate friend, "perfectly horrid. The idea of sleeping in a showerbath, and eating your breakfast from a tin plate, just for sake of catching a few silly fish! Why not send your guides out to get them for you?"

But, in spite of this profession of obstinate heresy, Beekman observed with secret joy that there were signs, before the end of the season, that Cornelia was drifting a little, a very little but still perceptibly, in the direction of a change of heart: She began to take an interest, as the big trout came along in September, in the reports of the catches made by the different anglers. She would saunter out with the other people to the corner of the porch to see the fish weighed and spread out on the grass. Several times she went with Beekman in the canoe to Hardscrabble Point, and showed distinct evidences of pleasure when he caught large trout. The last day of the season, when he returned from a successful expedition to Roach River and Lily Bay, she inquired with some particularity about the results of his sport; and in the evening, as the company sat before the great open fire in the hall of the hotel, she was heard to use this information with considerable skill in putting down Mrs. Minot Peabody of Boston, who was recounting the details of her husband's catch at Spencer Pond. Cornelia was not a person to be contented with the back seat, even in fish-stories.

When Beekman observed these indications he was much encouraged, and resolved to push his educational experiment briskly forward to his customary goal of success.

"Some things can be done, as well as others," he said in his masterful way, as three of us were walking home together after the autumnal dinner of the Petrine Club, which he always attended as a graduate member. "A real fisherman never gives up. I told you I'd make an angler out of my wife; and so I will. It has been rather difficult. She is 'dour' in rising. But she's beginning to take notice of the fly now. Give me another season, and I'll have her landed."

Good old Beekman! Little did he think— But I must not interrupt the story with moral reflections.

The preparations that he made for his final effort at conversion were thorough and prudent. He had a private interview with Dewlap in regard to the construction of a practical fishing-costume for a lady, which resulted in something more reasonable and workmanlike than had ever been turned out by that famous artist. He ordered from Hook & Catchett a lady's angling-outfit of the most enticing description—a split-bamboo rod, light as a girl's wish and strong as a matron's will; an oxidized silver reel, with a monogram on one side, and a sapphire set in the handle for good luck; a book of flies, of all sizes and colours, with the correct names inscribed in gilt letters on each page. He surrounded his favorite sort with an aureole of elegance and beauty. And then he took Cornelia in September to the Upper Dam at Rangeley.

She went reluctant. She arrived disgusted. She stayed incredulous. She returned— Wait a bit, and you shall hear how she returned.

The Upper Dam at Rangeley is the place, of all others in the world, where the lunacy of angling may be seen in its incurable stage. There is a cosy little inn, called a camp, at the foot of a big lake. In front of the inn is a huge dam of gray stone, over which the river plunges into a great oval pool, where the trout assemble in the early fall to perpetuate their race. From the tenth of September to the thirtieth, there is not an hour of the day or night when there are no boats floating on that pool, and no anglers trailing the fly across its waters. Before the late fishermen are ready to come in at midnight, the early fishermen may be seen creeping down to the shore with lanterns in order to begin before cock-crow. The number of fish taken is not large—perhaps five or six for the whole company on an average day—but the size is sometimes enormous—nothing under three pounds is counted—and they pervade thought and conversation at the Upper Dam to the exclusion of every other subject. There is no driving, no dancing, no golf, no tennis. There is nothing to do but fish or die.

At first, Cornelia thought she would choose the latter alternative. But a remark of that skilful and morose old angler, McTurk, which she overheard on the verandah after supper, changed her mind.

"Women have no sporting instinct," said he. "They only fish because they see men doing it. They are imitative animals."

That same night she told Beekman, in the subdued tone which the architectural construction of the house imposes upon all confidential communications in the bedrooms, but with resolution in every accent, that she proposed to go fishing with him on the morrow.

"But not on that pool, right in front of the house, you understand. There must be some other place, out on the lake, where we can fish for three or four days, until I get the trick of this wobbly rod. Then I'll show that old bear, McTurk, what kind of an animal woman is."

Beekman was simply delighted. Five days of diligent practice at the mouth of Mill Brook brought his pupil to the point where he pronounced her safe.

"Of course," he said patronizingly, "you haven't learned all about it yet. That will take years. But you can get your fly out thirty feet, and you can keep the tip of your rod up. If you do that, the trout will hook himself, in rapid water, eight times out of ten. For playing him, if you follow my directions, you'll be all right. We will try the pool to-night, and hope for a medium-sized fish."

Cornelia said nothing, but smiled and nodded. She had her own thoughts.

At about nine o'clock Saturday night, they anchored their boat on the edge of the shoal where the big eddy swings around, put out the lantern and began to fish. Beekman sat in the bow of the boat, with his rod over the left side; Cornelia in the stern, with her rod over the right side. The night was cloudy and very black. Each of them had put on the largest possible fly, one a "Bee-Pond" and the other a "Dragon"; but even these were invisible. They measured out the right length of line, and let the flies drift back until they hung over the shoal, in the curly water where the two currents meet.

There were three other boats to the left of them. McTurk was their only neighbour in the darkness on the right. Once they heard him swearing softly to himself, and knew that he had hooked and lost a fish.

Away down at the tail of the pool, dimly visible through the gloom, the furtive fisherman, Parsons, had anchored his boat. No noise ever came from that craft. If he wished to change his position, he did not pull up the anchor and let it down again with a bump. He simply lengthened or shortened his anchor rope. There was no click of the reel when he played a fish. He drew in and paid out the line through the rings by hand, without a sound. What he thought when a fish got away, no one knew, for he never said it. He concealed his angling as if it had been a conspiracy. Twice that night they heard a faint splash in the water near his boat, and twice they saw him put his arm over the side in the darkness and bring it back again very quietly.

"That's the second fish for Parsons," whispered Beekman, "what a secretive old Fortunatus he is! He knows more about fishing than any man on the pool, and talks less."

Cornelia did not answer. Her thoughts were all on the tip of her own rod. About eleven o'clock a fine, drizzling rain set in. The fishing was very slack. All the other boats gave it up in despair; but Cornelia said she wanted to stay out a little longer, they might as well finish up the week.

At precisely fifty minutes past eleven, Beekman reeled up his line, and remarked with firmness that the holy Sabbath day was almost at hand and they ought to go in.

"Not till I've landed this trout," said Cornelia.

"What? A trout! Have you got one?"

"Certainly; I've had him on for at least fifteen minutes. I'm playing him Mr. Parsons' way. You might as well light the lantern and get the net ready; he's coming in towards the boat now."

Beekman broke three matches before he made the lantern burn; and when he held it up over the gunwale, there was the trout sure enough, gleaming ghostly pale in the dark water, close to the boat, and quite tired out. He slipped the net over the fish and drew it in—a monster.

"I'll carry that trout, if you please," said Cornelia, as they stepped out of the boat; and she walked into the camp, on the last stroke of midnight, with the fish in her hand, and quietly asked for the steelyard.

Eight pounds and fourteen ounces—that was the weight. Everybody was amazed. It was the "best fish" of the year. Cornelia showed no sign of exultation, until just as John was carrying the trout to the icehouse. Then she flashed out: "Quite a fair imitation, Mr. McTurk—isn't it?"

Now McTurk's best record for the last fifteen years was seven pounds and twelve ounces.

So far as McTurk is concerned, this is the end of the story. But not for the De Peysters. I wish it were. Beekman went to sleep that night with a contended spirit. He felt that his experiment in education had been a success. He had made his wife an angler.

He had indeed, and to an extent which he little suspected. That Upper Dam trout was to her like the first taste of blood to the tiger. It seemed to change, at once, not so much her character as the direction of her vital energy. She yielded to the lunacy of angling, not by slow degrees (as first a transient delusion, then a fixed idea, then a chronic infirmity, finally a mild insanity), but by a sudden plunge into the most violent mania. So far from being ready to die at Upper Dam, her desire now was to live there—and to live solely for the sake of fishing—as long as the season was open.

There were two hundred and forty hours left to midnight on the thirtieth of September. At least two hundred of these she spent on the pool; and when Beekman was too exhausted to manage the boat and the net and the lantern for her, she engaged a trustworthy guide to take Beekman's place while he slept. At the end of the last day her score was twenty-three, with an average of five pounds and a quarter. His score was nine, with an average of four pounds. He had succeeded far beyond his wildest hopes.

The next year his success became even more astonishing. They went to the Titan Club in Canada. The ugliest and most inaccessible sheet of water in that territory is Lake Pharaoh.

But it is famous for the extraordinary fishing at a certain spot near the outlet, where there is just room enough for one canoe. They camped on Lake Pharaoh for six weeks, by Mrs. De Peyster's command; and her canoe was always the first to reach the fishing-ground in the morning, and the last to leave it in the evening.

Someone asked him, when he returned to the city, whether he had good luck.

"Quite fair," he tossed off in a careless way; "we took over three hundred pounds."

"To your own rod?" asked the inquirer, in admiration.

"No-o-o," said Beekman, "there were two of us."

There were two of them, also, the following year, when they joined the Natasheebo Salmon Club and fished that celebrated river in Labrador. The custom of drawing lots every night for the water that each member was to angle over the next day, seemed to be especially designed to fit the situation. Mrs. De Peyster could fish her own pool and her husband's too. The result of that year's fishing was something phenomenal. She had a score that made a paragraph in the newspapers and called out editorial comment. One editor was so inadequate to the situation as to entitle the article in which he described her triumph "The Equivalence of Woman." It was well-meant, but she was not at all pleased with it.

She was now not merely an angler, but a "record" angler of the most virulent type. Wherever they went, she wanted, and she got, the pick of the water. She seemed to be equally at home on all kinds of streams, large and small. She would pursue the little mountain-brook trout in the early spring, and the Labrador salmon in July, and the huge speckled trout of the northern lakes in September, with the same avidity and resolution. All that she cared for was to get the best and the most of the fishing at each place where she angled. This she always did.

And Beekman—well, for him there were no more long separations from the partner of his life while he went off to fish some favourite stream. There were no more home-comings after a good day's sport to find her clad in cool and dainty raiment on the verandah, ready to welcome him with friendly badinage. There was not even any casting of the fly around Hardscrabble Point while she sat in the canoe reading a novel, looking up with mild and pleasant interest when he caught a larger fish than usual, as an older and wiser person looks at a child playing some innocent game. Those days of a divided interest between man and wife were gone. She was now fully converted, and more. Beekman and Cornelia were one; and she was the one.

The last time I saw the De Peysters he was following her along the Beaverkill, carrying a landing-net and a basket, but no rod. She paused for a moment to exchange greetings, and then strode on down the stream. He lingered for a few minutes longer to light a pipe.

"Well, old man," I said, "you certainly have succeeded in making an angler of Mrs. De Peyster."

"Yes, indeed," he answered—"haven't I?" Then he continued, after a few thoughtful puffs of smoke. "Do you know, I'm not quite so sure as I used to be that fishing is the best of all sports. I sometimes think of giving it up and going in for croquet."

The Lady or the Salmon?

Andrew Lang

THE CIRCUMSTANCES THAT ATTENDED AND CAUSED THE
death of the Hon. Houghton Grannom have not long been
known to me, and it is only now that, by the decease of his
father, Lord Whitchurch, and the extinction of his noble
family, I am permitted to divulge the facts. That the true tale
of my unhappy friend will touch different chords in different
breasts, I am well aware. The sportsman, I think, will hesitate
to approve him; the fair, I hope, will absolve. Who are we, to
scrutinize human motives, and to award our blame to actions
that, perhaps, might have been our own, had opportunity
beset and temptation beguiled us? There is a certain point at
which the keenest sense of honor, the most chivalrous affection and devotion, cannot bear the strain, but break like a
salmon line under a masterful stress. That my friend suc-
cumbed, I admit, that he was his own judge, the severest,
and passed and executed sentence on himself, I have now to
show.

I shall never forget the shock with which I read in the
Scotsman, under "Angling," the following paragraph:

Tweed.—Strange Death of an Angler.— An unfortunate event has cast a gloom over fishers in this district. As Mr. K—, the keeper on the B— water, was busy angling yesterday, his attention was caught by some object floating on the stream. He cast his flies over it, and landed a soft felt hat, the ribbon stuck full of salmon flies. Mr. K— at once hurried upstream, filled with the most lively apprehensions. These were soon justified. In a shallow, below the narrow, deep and dangerous rapids called the Trows, Mr. K— saw a salmon leaping in a very curious manner. On a closer examination, he found that the fish was attached to a line. About seventy yards higher he found, in shallow water, the body of a man, the hand still grasping in death the butt of the rod, to which the salmon was fast, all the line being run out. Mr. K— at once rushed into the stream, and dragged out the body, in which he recognized with horror the Hon. Houghton Grannom, to whom the water was lately let. Life had been for some minutes extinct, and though Mr. K— instantly hurried for Dr. —, that gentleman could only attest the melancholy fact. The wading in the Trows is extremely dangerous and difficult, and Mr. Grannom, who was fond of fishing without an attendant, must have lost his balance, slipped, and been dragged down by the weight of his waders. The recent breaking off of the hon. gentleman's contemplated marriage on the very wedding-day will be fresh in the memory of our readers.

This was the story which I read in the newspaper during breakfast one morning in November. I was deeply grieved, rather than astonished, for I have often remonstrated with poor Grannom on the recklessness of his wading. It was with some surprise that I received, in the course of the day, a letter from him, in which he spoke only of indifferent matters, of the fishing which he had taken, and so forth. The letter was accompanied, however, by a parcel. Tearing off the outer cover, I found a sealed document addressed to me, with the super-scription, "Not to be opened until after my father's decease." This injunction, of course, I have scrupulously obeyed. The death of Lord Whitchurch, the last of the Grannoms, now gives me liberty to publish my friend's *Apologia pro morte et vita sua.*

Dear Smith [the document begins], Before you read this—long before, I hope—I shall have solved the great mystery—if, indeed, we solve it. If the water runs down tomorrow, and there is every prospect that it will do so, I must have the opportunity of making such an end as even malignity cannot suspect of being voluntary. There are plenty of fish in the water; if I hook one in the Trows, I shall let myself go whither the current takes me. Life has for weeks been odious to me; for what is life without honor, without love, and coupled with shame and remorse? Repentance I cannot call the emotion which gnaws me at the heart, for in similar circumstances (unlikely as these are to occur) I feel that I would do the same thing again.

Are we but automata, worked by springs, moved by the stronger impulse, and unable to choose for ourselves which impulse that shall be? Even now, in decreeing my own destruction, do I exercise free will, or am I the sport of hereditary tendencies, of mistaken views of honor, of seeming self-sacrifice, which, perhaps, is but selfishness in disguise? I blight my unfortunate father's old age; I destroy the last of an ancient house; but I remove from the path of Olive Dunne the shadow that must rest upon the sunshine of what will eventually, I trust, be a happy life, unvexed by memories of one who loved her passionately: Dear Olive! How pure, how ardent was my devotion to her none knows better than you. But Olive had, I will not say a fault, though I suffer from it, but a quality, or rather two qualities, which have completed my misery. Lightly as she floats on the stream of society, the most casual observer, and even the enamored beholder, can see that Olive Dunne has great pride, and no sense of humor. Her dignity is her idol. What makes her, even for a moment, the possible theme of ridicule is in her eyes an unpardonable sin. This sin, I must with penitence confess, I did indeed commit. Another woman might have forgiven me. I know not how that may be; I throw myself on the mercy of the court. But, if another could pity and pardon, to Olive this was impossible. I have never seen her since that fatal moment when, paler than her orange blossoms, she swept through the porch of the church, while I, disheveled, mud-stained, half-drowned—ah! that memory will torture me if memory at all remains. And yet, fool, maniac, that I was, I could not resist the wild, mad impulse to laugh, which shook the rustic spectators, and which in my case was due, I trust, to hysterical but not unmanly emotion. If any woman, any bride, could forgive such an apparent but most unintentional insult, Olive Dunne, I knew, was not that woman. My abject letters of explanation, my appeals for mercy, were returned unopened. Her parents pitied me, perhaps had reasons for being on my side, but Olive was of marble. It is not only myself that she cannot pardon, she will never, I know, forgive herself while my existence reminds her of what she had to endure. When she receives the intelligence of my demise, no suspicion will occur to her; she will not say "He is fitly punished"; but her peace of mind will gradually return.

It is for this, mainly, that I sacrifice myself, but also because I cannot endure the dishonor of a laggard in love and a recreant bridegroom.

So much for my motives: now to my tale.

The day before our wedding day had been the happiest of my life. Never had I felt so certain of Olive's affections, never so fortunate in my own. We parted in the soft moonlight; she, no doubt to finish her nuptial preparations; I, to seek my couch in the little rural inn above the roaring waters of the Budon.[1]

---

[1] From motives of delicacy I suppress the true name of the river.

Move eastward, happy earth, and leave
　　Yon orange sunset fading slow;
　　From fringes of the faded eve
　　Oh, happy planet, eastward go,
I murmured, though the atmospheric conditions were not really
those described by the poet.

　　Ah, bear me with thee, smoothly borne,
　　Dip forward under starry light,
　　And move me to my marriage morn,
　　And round again to—

"River in grand order, sir" said the voice of Robins,
the keeper, who recognized me in the moonlight. "There's
a regular monster in the Ashweil," he added, naming a
favorite cast; "never saw nor heard of such a fish in the
water before."

"Mr. Dick must catch him, Robins," I answered; "no
fishing for me tomorrow."

"No, sir," said Robins, affably. "Wish you joy, sir, and
Miss Olive, too. It's a pity, though! Master Dick, he throws
a fine fly, but he gets flurried with a big fish, being young.
And this one is a topper."

With that he gave me goodnight, and I went to bed,
but not to sleep. I was fevered with happiness; the past
and future reeled before my wakeful vision. I heard every
clock strike; the sounds of morning were astir, and still I
could not sleep. The ceremony, for reasons connected with
our long journey to my father's place in Hampshire, was to

be early—half-past ten was the hour. I looked at my watch; it was seven of the clock, and then I looked out of the window: it was a fine, soft, gray morning, with a south wind tossing the yellowing boughs. I got up, dressed in a hasty way, and thought I would just take a look at the river. It was, indeed, in glorious order, lapping over the top of the sharp stone which we regarded as a measure of the due size of water.

The morning was young, sleep was out of the question; I could not settle my mind to read. Why should I not take a farewell cast, alone, of course? I always disliked the attendance of a gillie. I took my salmon rod out of its case, rigged it up, and started for the stream, which flowed within a couple of hundred yards of my quarters. There it raced under the ash tree, a pale delicate brown, perhaps a little thing too colored. I therefore put on a large Silver Doctor, and began steadily fishing down the ash tree cast. What if I should wipe Dick's eye, I thought, when, just where the rough and smooth water meet, there boiled up a head and shoulders such as I had never seen on any fish. My heart leaped and stood still, but there came no sensation from the rod, and I finished the cast, my knees actually trembling beneath me. Then I gently lifted the line, and very elaborately tested every link of the powerful casting line. Then I gave him ten minutes by my watch; next, with unspeakable emotion, I stepped into the stream and repeated the cast. Just at the same spot he came up again; the huge rod bent like a switch, and the salmon rushed straight down the pool, as if he meant to make for the sea. I staggered on to dry land to follow him the easier, and dragged at my watch to time the fish; a quarter to eight. But the slim chain had broken, and the watch, as I hastily thrust it back, missed my pocket and fell into the water. There was no time to stoop for it; the fish started afresh, tore up the pool as fast as he had gone down it, and, rushing behind the torrent, into the eddy at the top, leaped clean out of the water. He was seventy pounds if he was an ounce. Here he slackened a little, dropping back, and I got in some line. Now he sulked so intensely that I thought he had got the line round a rock. It might be broken, might be holding fast to a sunken stone, for aught that I could tell; and the time was passing, I knew not how rapidly. I tried all known methods, tugging at him, tapping the butt, and slackening line on him. At last the top of the rod was slightly agitated, and then, back flew the long line in my face. Gone! I reeled up with a sigh, but the line tightened again. He had made a sudden rush under my bank, but there he lay again like a stone. How long? Ah! I cannot tell how long! I heard the church clock strike, but missed the number of strokes. Soon he started again downstream into the shallows, leaping at the end of his rush—the monster. Then he came slowly up, and "jiggered" savagely at the line. It seemed impossible that any tackle could stand these short violent jerks. Soon he showed signs of weakening. Once his huge silver side *appeared for a moment near the surface, but he retreated to his old fastness. I was in a tremor of delight and despair. I should have thrown down my rod, and flown on the wings of love to Olive and the altar. But I hoped that there was time still—that it was not so very late! At length he was failing. I heard ten o'clock strike. He came up and lumbered on the surface of the pool. Gradually I drew him, plunging ponderously, to the graveled beach, where I meant to "tail" him. He yielded to the strain, he was in the shallows, the line was shortened. I stooped to seize him. The frayed and overworn gut broke at a knot, and with a loose roll he dropped back toward the deep. I sprang at him, stumbled, fell on him, struggled with him, but he slipped from my arms. In that moment I knew more than the anguish of Orpheus. Orpheus! Had I, too, lost my Eurydice? I rushed from the stream, up the steep bank, along to my rooms. I passed the church door. Olive, pale as her orange blossoms, was issuing from the porch. The clock pointed to 10:45. I was ruined, I knew it, and I laughed. I laughed like a lost spirit. She swept past me, and, amidst the amazement of the gentle and simple, I sped wildly away. Ask me no more. The rest is silence.*

Thus ends my hapless friend's narrative. I leave it to the judgment of women and of men. Ladies, would you have acted as Olive Dunne acted? Would pride or pardon, or mirth have ridden sparkling in your eyes? Men, my brethren, would ye have deserted the salmon for the lady, or the lady for the salmon? I know what I would have done had I been fair Olive Dunne. What I would have done had I been Houghton Grannom I may not venture to divulge. For this narrative, then, as for another, "Let every man read it as he will, and every woman as the gods have given her wit."[2]

---

[2] After this paper was in print, an angler was actually drowned while engaged in playing a salmon. This unfortunate circumstance followed, and did not suggest the composition of the story.

A Stream for Anglers

W. H. H. Murray

I KNOW A STREAM AMONG THE HILLS, WHICH GLIDES DOWN
steep declines, flows across level stretches and tumbles over
rocky verges into dark ravines. Over it are white birches, and
firs, and fragrant cedars, some spruces, tall and straight, and
here and there an oak or mountain ash. The breezes, born of
cool currents that pour downward from upper heights, where
snow whitens yet, blow along this stream among the mountains full of ozone, brewed in the upper atmospheres, and
which the nose of the climber drinks as the Homeric gods
drank their wine, leisurely, because it is so strong and pure.
In the spruces along this stream live two big, brown owls that
doze through the day, and if you will sit for an hour and listen you will hear them mutter and murmur in their dreams;
dreaming of mice in the meadow, and young chickens in the
lowlands, I fancy. On the largest oak, old and gnarled, at the
end of a dead bough, a white-headed eagle sits watchfully.
Twenty feet below him his mate is hovering over four eggs in
a huge nest made of dry sticks. Their eyes have seen more suns
rise and set than mine, and will see the crimson long after

mine are closed forever, doubtless. All men are their foes, yet they live on. All men are my friends, still I must die. Queer, isn't it?

There are anglers on this mountain stream, but only I know them. They fish each day, and each day fill their creels, and yet they use no rods, nor lines, nor hooks, nor flies, nor bait. It is because I have never fished this hidden stream myself that I have seen them fish it. Poachers? Nay. This brook is their preserve, and I would be a poacher on their rights should I cast line across it. Who are these strange anglers that angle so strangely?

The oldest of them is a snapping turtle, and a great angler he is in truth. I ambushed him as he lay asleep on a log one day, and on his back was written, A.D. 1710. That makes him one hundred and eighty years old—an age that all good anglers ought to live to. Do you tell me "That was a lie; he couldn't be so old?" It may be so—I won't quarrel with you, friend. Regard it as a bit of history, and I will agree with you. But he is a great angler, this old turtle, and has caught more trout than any angler who reads this passage—ten to one, I warrant.

The best angler of them all—better than the water-snake or the kingfisher, or the mountain cat, or the turtle, wise as he is—is an old brown mink. He is so old that his face is gray and his fur shabby, but he is a wise old angler. Six days I watched him come to the stream, and six good half-pound trout did I see the old gray veteran sit and eat on the cool, damp ledge against which the whirling bubbles ran. It was a sight to see him wash himself after his repast! And after he had thoroughly washed his mouth and cleansed his hands, he would stand and look into the deep, dark pool for a moment, contemplatively, as I fancied. Perhaps he is a deacon among the minks! Who knows? Isn't a good angler as good as a deacon, anyway?

There is a bit of meadow on the stream enclosed with a fringe of white birches and cedar growths; and amid the green grasses of it are cranberry vines, and bunches of beaver cups; white and blue flowers speck it with color, and the earth odors are strong over it. It is pleasant to stand in it and breathe in the aboriginal scents of wild roots and uncultivated mould. The untameable in me fraternizes so lovingly with this rare bit of untamed nature. This little mountain meadow, from whose stretch the beaver, with their sharp teeth, cut the trees centuries ago, is so real and genuine that it charges its influence to the very core of me. It is so natural that it makes me more so.

The old beaver dam is still there, and over it the water pours with soft noises into a deep and wide pool. On one side of this dark bit of water is a great rock. Its front is covered with thick mosses very rich in color. Across it wanders a vine with little red berries strung on it. Can you see the old beaver dam, the pool, the big rock, the moss, the running vine and the shining red berries? Yes? Very likely you can; but, oh, you who have such eyes to see—you cannot see the huge trout whose home that dark, deep pool is, and which I have seen so many times as he rose for the bug or grub that I tossed him. And once as

I lay on the edge of the pool, hidden in the long grasses, I saw him at play, having a frolic all by himself, and, oh, he made that space of gloomy water iridescent as he flashed and flew through it. Where is he? Do you really wish to know? Well, I will be good and tell you. He is where I found him.

On Dry-Cow Fishing
As A Fine Art

Rudyard Kipling

IT MUST BE CLEARLY UNDERSTOOD THAT I AM NOT AT ALL proud of this performance. In Florida men sometimes hook and land, on rod and tackle a little finer than a steam-crane and chain, a mackerel-like fish called "tarpon," which sometime run to 120 pounds. Those men stuff their captures and exhibit them in glass cases and become puffed up. On the Columbia River sturgeon of 150 pounds weight are taken with the line. When the sturgeon is hooked the line is fixed to the nearest pine tree or steamboat-wharf, and after some hours or days the sturgeon surrenders himself, if the pine or the line do not give way. The owner of the line then states on oath that he has caught a sturgeon, and he, too, becomes proud.

These things are mentioned to show how light a creel will fill the soul of a man with vanity. I am not proud. It is nothing to me that I have hooked and played seven hundred pounds weight of quarry. All my desire is to place the little affair on record before the mists of memory breed the miasma of exaggeration.

The minnow cost eighteenpence. It was a beautiful quill minnow, and the tackle-maker said that it could be thrown as a fly. He guaranteed further in respect to the triangles—it glittered with triangles—that, if necessary, the minnow would hold a horse. A man who speaks too much truth is just as offensive as a man who speaks too little. None the less, owing to the defective condition of the present law of libel, the tackle-maker's name must be withheld.

The minnow and I and a rod went down to a brook to attend to a small jack who lived between two clumps of flags in the most cramped swim that he could select. As a proof that my intentions were strictly honourable, I may mention that I was using a light split-cane rod—very dangerous if the line runs through weeds, but very satisfactory in clean water, inasmuch as it keeps a steady strain on the fish and prevents him from taking liberties. I had an old score against the jack. He owed me two live-bait already, and I had reason to suspect him of coming up-stream and interfering with a little bleak-pool under a horse-bridge which lay entirely beyond his sphere of legitimate influence. Observe, therefore, that my tackle and my motives pointed clearly to jack, and jack alone; though I knew that there were monstrous big perch in the brook.

The minnow was thrown as a fly several times, and, owing to my peculiar, and hitherto unpublished, methods of fly throwing, nearly six pennyworth of the triangles came off, either in my coat-collar, or my thumb, or the back of my hand. Fly fishing is a very gory amusement.

The jack was not interested in the minnow, but towards twilight a boy opened a gate of the field and let in some twenty or thirty cows and half-a-dozen cart-horses, and they were all very much interested. The horses galloped up and down the field and shook the banks, but the cows walked solidly and breathed heavily, as people breathe who appreciate the Fine Arts.

By this time I had given up all hope of catching my jack fairly, but I wanted the live-bait and bleak-account settled before I went away, even if I tore up the bottom of the brook. Just before I had quite made up my mind to borrow a tin of chloride of lime from the farm-house—another triangle had fixed itself in my fingers—I made a cast which for pure skill, exact judgement of distance, and perfect coincidence of hand and eye and brain, would have taken every prize at a bait-casting tournament. That was the first half of the cast. The second was postponed because the quill minnow would not return to its proper place, which was under the lobe of my left ear. It had done thus before, and I supposed it was in collision with a grass tuft, till I turned round and saw a large red and white bald faced cow trying to rub what would be withers in a horse with her nose. She looked at me reproachfully, and her look said as plainly as words: "The season is too far advanced for gadflies. What is this strange disease?"

I replied, "Madam, I must apologize for an unwarrantable liberty on the part of my minnow, but if you will have the goodness to keep still until I can reel in, we will adjust this little difficulty."

I reeled in very swiftly and cautiously, but she would not wait. She put her tail in the air and ran away. It was a purely involuntary motion on my part: I struck. Other anglers may contradict me, but I firmly believe that if a man had foul-hooked his best friend through the nose, and that friend ran, the man would strike by instinct. I struck, therefore, and the reel began to sing just as merrily as though I had caught my jack. But had it been a jack, the minnow would have come away. I told the tackle-maker this much afterwards, and he laughed and made allusions to the guarantee about holding a horse.

Because it was a fat innocent she-cow that had done me no harm the minnow held—held like an anchor-fluke in coral moorings—and I was forced to dance up and down an inter-minable field very largely used by cattle. It was like salmon fishing in a nightmare. I took gigantic strides, and every stride found me up to my knees in marsh. But the cow seemed to skate along the squashy green by the brook, to skim over the miry backwaters, and to float like a mist through the patches of rush that squirted black filth over my face. Sometimes we whirled through a mob of her friends—there were no friends to help me—and they looked scandalized; and sometimes a young and frivolous cart-horse would join in the chase for a few miles, and kick solid pieces of mud into my eyes; and through all the mud, the milky smell of kine, the rush and the smother, I was aware of my own voice crying: "Pussy, pussy, pussy! Pretty pussy! Come along then, puss-cat!" You see it is so hard to speak to a cow properly, and she would not listen—no, she would not listen.

Then she stopped, and the moon got up behind the pollards to tell the cows to lie down; but they were all on their feet, and they came trooping to see. And she said, "I haven't had my supper, and I want to go to bed, and please don't worry me." And I said, "The matter has passed beyond any apology. There are three courses open to you, my dear lady. If you'll have the common sense to walk up to my creel I'll get my knife and you shall have all the minnow. Or, again, if you'll let me move across to your near side, instead of keeping me so coldly on your off side, the thing will come away in one tweak. I can't pull it out over your withers. Better still, go to a post and rub it out, dear. It won't hurt much, but if you think I'm going to lose my rod to please you, you are mistaken." And she said, "I don't understand what you are saying. I am very, very unhappy." And I said, "It's all your fault for trying to fish. Do go to the nearest gate-post, you nice fat thing, and rub it out."

For a moment I fancied she was taking my advice. She ran away and I followed. But all the other cows came with us in a bunch, and I thought of Phaeton trying to drive the Chariot of the Sun, and Texan cowboys killed by stampeding cattle, and "*Green Grow the Rushes O!*" and Solomon and Job, and "loosing the bands of Orion," and hooking Behemoth, and Wordsworth who talks about whirling round with stones and rocks and trees, and "Here we go round the Mulberry Bush," and "Pippin Hill," and "Hey Diddle Diddle," and most especially the top joint of my rod. Again she stopped—but nowhere in the neighborhood of my knife—and her sisters stood moonfaced round her. It seemed that she might, now, run towards me, and I looked for a tree, because cows are very different from salmon, who only jump against the line, and never molest the fisherman. What followed was worse than any direct attack. She began to buck-jump, to stand on her head and her tail alternately, to leap into the sky, all four feet together, and to dance on her hind legs. It was so violent and improper, so desperately unladylike, that I was inclined to blush, as one would blush at the sight of a prominent statesman sliding down a fire escape, or a duchess chasing her cook with a skillet. That flopsome *abandon* might go on all night in the lonely meadow among the mists, and if it went on all night—this was pure inspiration—I might be able to worry through the fishing line with my teeth.

Those who desire an entirely new sensation should chew with all their teeth, and against time, through a best water-proofed silk line, one end of which belongs to a mad cow dancing fairy rings in the moonlight; at the same time keeping one eye on the cow and the other on the top joint of a split-cane rod. She buck-jumped and I bit on the slack just in front of the reel; and I am in a position to state that that line was cored with steel wire throughout the particular section which I attacked. This has been formally denied by the tackle-maker, who is not to be believed.

The *wheep* of the broken line running through the rings told me that henceforth the cow and I might be strangers. I had already bidden good-bye to some tooth or teeth; but no price is too great for freedom of the soul.

"Madam," I said, "the minnow and twenty feet of very superior line are your alimony without reservation. For the wrong I have unwittingly done to you I express my sincere regret. At the same time, may I hope that Nature, the kindest of nurses, will in due season—"

She or one of her companions must have stepped on her spare end of the line in the dark, for she bellowed wildly and ran away, followed by all the cows. I hoped the minnow was disengaged at last; and before I went away looked at my watch, fearing to find it nearly midnight. My last cast for the jack was made at 6:23 p.m. There lacked still three and a-half minutes of the half-hour; and I would have sworn that the moon was paling before the dawn!

———

"Simminly someone were chasing they cows down to bottom o' Ten Acre," said the farmer that evening. "'Twasn't you, sir?"

"Now under what earthly circumstances do you suppose I should chase your cows? I wasn't fishing for them, was I?"

Then all the farmer's family gave themselves up to jam-smeared laughter for the rest of the evening, because that was a rare and precious jest, and it was repeated for months, and the fame of it spread from that farm to another, and yet another at least three miles away, and it will be used again for the benefit of visitors when the freshets come down in spring.

But to the greater establishment of my honour and glory I submit in print this bald statement of fact, that I may not, through forgetfulness, be tempted later to tell how I hooked a bull on a Marlow Buzz, how he ran up a tree and took to water, and how I played him along the London-road for thirty miles, and gaffed him at Smithfield. Errors of this kind may creep in with the lapse of years, and it is my ambition ever to be a worthy member of that fraternity who pride themselves on never deviating by one hair's breadth from the absolute and literal truth.

A Bit of Luck

Harry Plunket Greene

I HAD AN EXPERIENCE WITH A TROUT ON THE KENNET, WHICH I always associate, quite undeservedly, with "snatching." It was in 1922, and I was staying with Mr. Giveen, who had taken the Mill fishing from Col. Grove-Hills for the latter half of the season. He and I had often stood on the bridge at the top, where the water falls down from the lake of Ramsbury Manor, and hungrily objurgated the great fat three-pounders which laughed at us from beneath. These were rovers by profession, and never stayed long enough in one place to be fished for individually from below; and were up to every trick from above. They would lie with their noses on the ledge immediately underneath us, and dreamily watch the smoke from our pipes ascending to the blue; but the moment the top of a rod appeared over the edge, off they went. We tried concerted action many times, but as soon as ever one of the watchers disappeared from the bridge the pool was abandoned to two-year-olds. On this occasion I was passing by the sluice which forms a small side-carrier to the main fall and I put my head casually over the side, expecting nothing, and there right below

175

me was a big golden trout tucked up under the boards, with his head down-stream and his tail up against the cracks where the water spurted through. He was doing no good there, so I felt it was my duty to get him.

It was an awful prospect. Immediately below him two planks ran across the sluice at intervals of about eight feet, and below them again in the fairway there was a veritable barricade of posts sticking up out of the stream in ragged profusion. There were three on the near side and two on the far side and a gaunt rubbing-post in the middle acting as a buoy, round which every sporting fish was in honor bound to double. Below these again there was another pole running right across the stream only four inches above the water, which swirled under it at a great pace. A more hopeless barbed-wire entanglement it would be hard to imagine to try and fish a fish out of, even if one hooked him. However, he was a beauty, and the fact that he was practically ungetable made it all the more exciting. I had up the ordinary tackle; by all the laws of caution I should have put up a ginger-quill with a No. 1 hook and a May-fly cast, but I reflected that if he got tangled up in the barriers a steel hawser would not hold him, and that if by some amazing fluke he ever came through, the fine tackle would be as good as anything else. Moreover, I should be able to swagger to the others about 4X casts and 000 hooks even more insupportably than before; so I stuck to what I had.

I stood well back where I could just see the tip of his nose and he could not see me, reeled in the line to within six inches of the cast, and gently dropped the fly on to him. It was at once carried out by the stream. I thought it was going to be hopeless, when to my intense delight the back eddy swirled it round at exactly the right moment and brought it over him again. It was then seized once more by the stream and carried off afresh. The process was repeated automatically without my having to do a thing, and there went my fly playing "last across" with him, rushing up the backwater, tweaking his nose and dashing off downstream before he could say a word. I was so delighted and laughing so hard that I could not help crawling up to see the fun, and put my head over to have a look. He was intently absorbed in the game and never saw me. He appeared to take no notice at first and treated it all with dignified unconcern, but as the impudent little beast dashed past him smothering him with insults he began to get impatient, and I saw his tail detach itself from the sluice-board and begin to wag. Then he began to shake his head and bunch himself to attack. But nothing happened for a long time and I was just going to give it up, as my arm was getting tired from the unnatural position, when I had a wonderful bit of luck. There was a twig sticking out from the wall on the far side over the back eddy, and the gut caught over it, and, before I knew it, there was the fly bobbing up and down in the water, right in front of him. This was too much. His enemy was delivered into his hands.

He leaped at it, seized it, knew in a moment what had happened, and dashed off down-stream under the planks and through the posts and out into the pool at the bottom. There

I had to leave him for a long time to settle himself, with my rod bent double under the first plank. Then the fun began. I cautiously passed it under this with one hand and retrieved it with the other and did the same with the second plank. All idea of keeping the line taut was perforce abandoned. I still had the six upright posts and the flat pole beyond to negotiate. If he once got tangled up in these it would be all over. He was near the top of the pool now, and I lay flat on the ground with the point of the rod out in the space between me and the centre post, terrified lest he should swim up on the near side of A post, catch sight of me, and dash down on the far side or pay a visit to X, Y or Z post. I clung to Mother Earth like a tiger-skin on a polished oak floor. Sure enough, up he came. He swam through the near channel and roamed about under my eyes (or the corner of one of them) for about a fortnight apparently, and then swam slowly back to the pool the same way he had come!

It was almost too good to be true! But the crux was still to be faced—there was still the flat pole to get under. It ran across the top of the pool, with a space of about four inches between it and the water. It was a bare two inches thick and it was quite rotten. I had to get the rod under it somehow (for I could never risk letting him out of the pool again), and I could only just reach it with my hand by holding on to the bank above with my toes and descending apoplectically towards the water. It cracked loudly the moment I touched it. I had to lean hard on the horrible thing with my right hand, pass the rod under with my left, scrabble it out again somehow with my right on the other side, change hands and work myself back up the bank. It groaned and shivered its timbers and fired off shots like a machine-gun—but the little iron-blue had squared it and it held. It was not all over even then, for if the fish had caught sight of me he would have dashed up through the uprights again; so I backed slowly out of sight into a withy-bed and stayed there till there was not a kick left in him. As a matter of fact, he had done it all for me by returning through the posts the same way he had come. The only credit I can take is for keeping out of sight and performing gymnastics with an almost superhuman skill for one of my size and weight. He weighed 2¼ lbs.

A Conference

Lewis Carroll

A CONFERENCE BETWIXT AN ANGLER, A HUNTER, AND A Professor; concerning angling, and the beautifying of Thomas his Quadrangle.

PISCATOR, VENATOR

PISCATOR. My honest Scholar, we are now arrived at the place whereof I spake, and trust me, we shall have good sport. How say you? Is not this a noble Quadrangle we see around us? And be not these lawns trimly kept, and this lake marvellous clear?

VENATOR. So marvellous clear, good Master, and withal so brief in compass, that methinks, if any fish of a reasonable bigness were therein, we must perforce espy it. I fear me there is none.

PISC. The less the fish, dear Scholar, the greater the skill in catching of it. Come, let's sit down, and, while we unpack the fishing-gear, I'll deliver a few remarks, both as to the fish to be met with hereabouts, and the properest method of fishing.

But you are to note first (for, as you are pleased to be my Scholar, it is fitting you should imitate my habits of close observation) that the margin of this lake is so deftly fashioned that each portion thereof is at one and the same distance from that tumulus which rises in the center.

VEN. O' my word 'tis so! You have indeed a quick eye, dear Master, and a wondrous readiness of observing.

PISC. Both may be yours in time, my Scholar, if with humility and patience you follow me as your model.

VEN. I thank you for that hope, great Master! But ere you begin your discourse, let me enquire of you one thing touching this noble Quadrangle,—Is all we see of a like antiquity? To be brief, think you that those two tall archways, that excavation in the parapet, and that quaint wooden box, belong to the ancient design of the building, or have men of our day thus sadly disfigured the place?

PISC. I doubt not they are new, dear Scholar. For indeed I was here but a few years since, and saw naught of these things. But what book is that I see lying by the water's edge?

VEN. A book of ancient ballads, and truly I am glad to see it, as we may herewith beguile the tediousness of the day, if our sport be poor, or if we grow weary.

PISC. This is well thought of. But now to business. And first I'll tell you somewhat of the fish proper to these waters. The Commoner kinds we may let pass: for though some of them be easily Plucked forth from the water, yet are they so slow, and withal have so little in them, that they are good for nothing, unless they be crammed up to the very eyes with such stuffing as comes readiest to hand. Of these the Stickleback, a mighty slow fish, is chiefest, and along with him you may reckon the Fluke, and divers others: All these belong to the "Mullet" genus, and be good to play, though scarcely worth examination.

I will now say somewhat of the Nobler kinds, and chiefly of the Gold-fish, which is a species highly thought of, and much sought after in these parts, not only by men, but by divers birds, as for example the King-fishers: And note that wheresoever you shall see those birds assemble, and but few insects about, there shall you ever find the Gold-fish most lively and richest in flavour: but wheresoever you perceive swarms of a certain gray fly, called the Dun-fly, there the Gold-fish are ever poorer in quality, and the King-fishers seldom seen.

A good Perch may sometimes be found hereabouts: but for a good fat Plaice (which is indeed but a magnified Perch) you may search these waters in vain. They that love such dainties must needs betake them to some distant Sea.

But for the manner of fishing, I would have you note first that your line be not thicker than an ordinary bell-rope: for look you, to flog the water, as though you laid on with a flail, is most preposterous, and will surely scare the fish. And note further, that your rod must by no means exceed ten, or at the most twenty, pounds in weight, for—

VEN. Pardon me, my Master, that thus break in on so excellent a discourse, but there now approaches us a Collegian, as I guess him to be, from whom we may haply learn the cause of these novelties we see around us.

[Here PISCATOR and VENATOR meet with a PRO-
FESSOR who, among other bits of wisdom, imparts the fact
that "even an English book, worth naught in this its native
dress, shall become, when rendered into German, a valuable
contribution to Science!"

Next, a "conference with one distraught: who discourseth
strangely of many things," i.e. a LUNATIC who "all the evening long saw lobsters marching around the table in unbroken
order."

And, finally . . .]

VENATOR. Oh me! Look you, Master! A fish, a fish!

PISCATOR. Then let us hook it.

[They hook it.]

A Fatal Salmon

Frank Forester

IT WAS AS FAIR A MORNING OF JULY AS EVER DAWNED IN THE blue summer sky; the sun as yet had risen but a little way above the waves of fresh green foliage which formed the horizon of the woodland scenery surrounding Widecomb Manor; and his heat, which promised ere mid-day to become excessive, was tempered now by the exhalations of the copious night-dews, and by the cool breath of the western breeze, which came down through the leafy gorges, in long, soft swells from the open moorlands.

All nature was alive and joyous; the air was vocal with the piping melody of the blackbirds and thrushes, carolling in every brake and bosky dingle; the smooth, green lawn before the windows of the old Hall was peopled with whole tribes of fat, lazy hares, limping about among the dewy herbage, fearless, as it would seem, of man's aggression; and to complete the picture, above, a score of splendid peacocks were strutting to and fro on the paved terraces, or perched upon the carved stone balustrades, displaying their gorgeous plumage to the early sunshine.

The shadowy mists of the first morning twilight had not been dispersed from the lower regions, and were suspended still in the middle air in broad fleecy masses, though melting rapidly away in the increasing warmth and brightness of the day.

And still a faint blue line hovered over the bed of the long rocky gorge, which divided the chase from the open country, floating about it like the steam of a seething caldron, and rising here and there into tall smoke-like columns, probably where some steeper cataract of the mountain-stream sent its foam skyward.

So early, indeed, was the hour, that had my tale been recited of these degenerate days, there would have been no gentle eyes awake to look upon the loveliness of new-awakened nature.

In the good days of old, however, when daylight was still deemed to be the fitting time for labor and for pastime, and night the appointed time for natural and healthful sleep, the dawn was wont to brighten beheld by other eyes than those of clowns and milkmaids, and the gay songs of the matutinal birds were listened to by ears that could appreciate their untaught melodies.

And now, just as the stable clock was striking four, the great oaken door of the old Hall was thrown open with a vigorous swing that made it rattle on its hinges, and Jasper St. Aubyn came bounding out into the fresh morning air, with a foot as elastic as that of the mountain roe, singing a snatch of some quaint old ballad.

He was dressed simply in a close-fitting jacket and tight hose of dark-green cloth, without any lace or embroidery, light boots of untanned leather, and a broad-leafed hat, with a single eagle's feather thrust carelessly through the band. He wore neither cloak nor sword, though it was a period at which gentlemen rarely went abroad without these, their distinctive attributes; but in the broad black belt which girt his rounded waist he carried a stout wood-knife with a buckhorn hilt; and over his shoulder there swung from a leathern thong a large wicker fishing-basket.

Nothing, indeed, could be simpler or less indicative of any particular rank or station in society than young St. Aubyn's garb, yet it would have been a very dull and unobservant eye which should take him for aught less than a high-born and high-bred gentleman.

His fine intellectual face, his bearing erect before heaven, the graceful ease of his every motion, as he hurried down the flagged steps of the terrace, and planted his light foot on the dewy greensward, all betokened gentle birth and gentle associations.

But he thought nothing of himself, nor cared for his advantages, acquired or natural. The long and heavy salmon-rod which he carried in his right hand, in three pieces as yet unconnected, did not more clearly indicate his purpose than the quick marking glance which he cast toward the half-veiled sun and hazy sky, scanning the signs of the weather.

"It will do, it will do," he said to himself, thinking as it were aloud, "for three or four hours at least; the sun will not shake off those vapors before eight o'clock at the earliest, and if he do come out then hot and strong, I do not know but the water is dark enough after the late rains to serve my turn a while longer. It will blow up, too, I think, from the westward, and there will be a brisk curl on the pools. But come, I must be moving, if I would reach Darringford to breakfast."

And as he spoke he strode out rapidly across the park toward the deep chasm of the stream, crushing a thousand aromatic perfumes from the dewy wild-flowers with his heedless foot, and thinking little of the beauties of nature, as he hastened to the scene of his loved exercise.

It was not long, accordingly, before he reached the brink of the steep rocky bank above the stream, which he proposed to fish that morning, and paused to select the best place for descending to the water's edge.

It was, indeed, as striking and romantic a scene as ever met the eye of painter or of poet. On the farther side of the gorge, scarcely a hundred yards distant, the dark limestone rocks rose sheer and precipitous from the very brink of the stream, rifted and broken into angular blocks and tall columnar masses, from the clefts of which, wherever they could find soil enough to support their scanty growth, a few stunted oaks shot out almost horizontally with their gnarled arms and dark-green foliage, and here and there the silvery bark and quivering tresses of the birch relieved the monotony of color by their gay brightness. Above, the cliffs were crowned with the beautiful purple heather, now in its very glow of summer bloom, about which were buzzing myriads of wild bees, sipping their nectar from its cups of amethyst.

The hither side, though rough and steep and broken, was not, in the place where Jasper stood, precipitous; indeed it seemed as if at some distant period a sort of landslip had occurred, by which the summit of the rocky wall had been broken into massive fragments, and hurled down in an inclined plane into the bed of the stream, on which it had encroached with its shattered blocks and rounded boulders.

Time, however, had covered all this abrupt and broken slope with a beautiful growth of oak and hazel coppice, among which, only at distant intervals, could the dun weather-beaten flanks of the great stones be discovered.

At the base of this descent, a hundred and fifty feet perhaps below the stand of the young sportsman, flowed the dark arrowy stream—a wild and perilous water. As clear as crystal, yet as dark as the brown cairngorm, it came pouring down among the broken rocks with a rapidity and force which showed what must be its fury when swollen by a storm among the mountains, here breaking into wreaths of rippling foam where some unseen ledge chafed its current, there roaring and surging white as December's snow among the great round-headed rocks, and there again wheeling in sullen eddies, dark and deceitful, round and round some deep rock-rimmed basin.

Here and there, indeed, it spread out into wide, shallow, rippling rapids, filling the whole bottom of the ravine from side to side, but more generally it did not occupy above a fourth part of the space below, leaving sometimes on this margin, sometimes on that, broad pebbly banks, or slaty ledges, affording an easy footing and a clear path to the angler in its troubled waters.

After a rapid glance over the well-known scene, Jasper plunged into the coppice, and following a faint track worn by the feet of the wild-deer in the first instance, and widened by his own bolder tread, soon reached the bottom of the chasm, though not until he had flushed from the dense oak covert two noble black cocks with their superb forked tails, and glossy purple-lustered plumage, which soared away, crowing their bold defiance, over the heathery moorlands.

Once at the water's edge, the young man's tackle was speedily made ready, and in a few minutes his long line went whistling through the air, as he wielded the powerful two-handed rod, as easily as if it had been a stripling's reed, and the large gaudy peacock-fly alighted on the wheeling eddies, at the tail of a long arrowy shoot, as gently as if it had settled from too long a flight. Delicately, deftly, it was made to dance and skim the clear, brown surface, until it had crossed the pool and neared the hither bank; then again, obedient to the pliant wrist, it arose on glittering wing, circled half around the angler's head, and was set fifteen yards aloof, straight as a wild bee's flight, into a little mimic whirlpool, scarce larger than the hat of the skilful fisherman, which spun round and round just to leeward of a gray ledge of limestone. Scarce had it reached its mark before the water broke all around it, and the gay deceit vanished, the heavy swirl of the surface, as the break was closing, indicating the great size of the fish which had risen. Just as the swirl was subsiding, and the forked tail of the monarch of the stream was half seen as he descended, that indescribable but well-known turn of the angler's wrist, fixed the barbed hook, and taught the scaly victim the nature of the prey he had gorged so heedlessly.

With a wild bound he threw himself three feet out of the water, showing his silver sides, with the sea-lice yet clinging to his scales, a fresh sea-run fish of fifteen, ay, eighteen pounds, and perhaps over.

On his broad back he strikes the water, but not as he meant the tightened line; for as he leaped the practised hand had lowered the rod's tip, that it fell in a loose bight below him. Again! again! again! and yet a fourth time he bounded into the air with desperate and vigorous *soubresaults*, like an unbroken steed that would dismount his rider, lashing the eddies of the dark stream into bright bubbling streaks, and making the heart of his captor beat high with anticipation of the desperate struggle that should follow, before the monster should lie panting and exhausted on the yellow sand or moist greensward.

Away! with the rush of an eagle through the air, he is gone like an arrow down the rapids—how the reel rings, and the line whistles from the swift working wheel; he is too swift, too headstrong to be checked as yet; tenfold the strength of that slender tackle might not control him in his first fiery rush.

But Jasper, although young in years, was old in the art, and skilful as the craftiest of the gentle craftsmen. He gives him the butt of his rod steadily, trying the strength of his tackle with a delicate and gentle finger, giving him line at every rush, yet firmly, cautiously, feeling his mouth all the while, and moderating his speed even while he yields to his fury.

Meanwhile, with the eye of intuition, and the nerve of iron, he bounds along the difficult shore, he leaps from rock to rock, alighting on their slippery tops with the firm agility of the rope-dancer, he splashes knee-deep through the slippery shallows, keeping his line ever taut, inclining his rod over his shoulder, bearing on his fish ever with a killing pull, steering him clear of every rock or stump against which he would fain smash the tackle, and landing him at length in a fine open roomy pool, at the foot of a long stretch of white and foamy rapids, down which he has just piloted him with the eye of faith, and the foot of instinct.

And now the great Salmon has turned sulky; like a piece of lead he has sunk to the bottom of the deep black pool, and lies on the gravel bottom in the sullenness of despair.

Jasper stooped, gathered up in his left hand a heavy pebble, and pitched it into the pool, as nearly as he could guess to the whereabouts of his game—another—and another! Aha! that last has roused him. Again he throws himself clear out of water, and again foiled in his attempt to smash the tackle, dashes away down stream impetuous.

But his strength is departing—the vigor of his rush is broken. The angler gives him the butt abundantly, strains on him with a heavier pull, yet ever yields a little as he exerts his failing powers; see, his broad, silver side has thrice turned up, even to the surface, and though each time he has recovered himself, each time it has been with a heavier and more sickly motion.

Brave fellow! his last race is run, his last spring sprung—no more shall he disport himself in the bright reaches of the Tamar; no more shall the Naiads wreathe his clear silver scales with river-greens and flowery rushes.

The cruel gaff is in his side—his cold blood stains the eddies for a moment—he flaps out his deathpang on the hard limestone.

"Who-whoop! a nineteen-pounder!"

Meantime the morning had worn onward, and ere the great fish was brought to the basket, the sun had soared clear above the mist-wreaths, and had risen so high into the summer heaven that his slant rays poured down into the gorge of the stream, and lighted up the clear depths with a lustre so transparent that every pebble at the bottom might have been discerned, with the large fish here and there floating mid-depth, with their heads upstream, their gills working with a quick motion, and their broad tails vibrating at short intervals slowly but powerfully, as they lay motionless in opposition to the very strongest of the swift current.

The breeze had died away, there was no curl upon the water, and the heat was oppressive.

Under such circumstances, to whip the stream was little better than mere loss of time, yet as he hurried with a fleet foot down the gorge, perhaps with some ulterior object, beyond the mere love of sport, Jasper at times cast his fly across the stream, and drew it neatly, and, as he thought, irresistibly, right over the recusant fish; but though once or twice a large lazy Salmon would sail up slowly from the depths, and almost touch the fly with his nose, he either sunk down slowly in disgust, without breaking the water, or flapped his broad tail over the shining fraud as if to mark his contempt.

It had now got to be near noon, for, in the ardor of his success, the angler had forgotten all about his intended breakfast; and, his first fish captured, had contented himself with a slender meal furnished from out his fishing-basket and his leathern bottle.

Jasper had traversed by this time some ten miles in length, following the sinuosities of the stream, and had reached a favorite pool at the head of a long, straight, narrow trench, cut by the waters themselves in the course of time, through the hard schistous rock which walls the torrent on each hand, not leaving the slightest ledge or margin between the rapids and the precipice.

Through this wild gorge of some fifty yards in length, the river shoots like an arrow over a steep inclined plane of limestone rock, the surface of which is polished by the action of the water, till it is as slippery as ice, and at the extremity leaps down a sheer descent of some twelve feet into a large, wide basin, surrounded by softly swelling banks of greensward, and a fair amphitheatre of woodland.

At the upper end this pool is so deep as to be vulgarly deemed unfathomable; below, however, it expands yet wider into a shallow rippling ford, where it is crossed by the high-road, down stream of which again there is another long, sharp rapid, and another fall, over the last steps of the hills; after which the nature of the stream becomes changed, and it murmurs gently onward through a green pastoral country, unrippled and uninterrupted.

Just in the inner angle of the high-road, on the right hand of the stream, there stood an old-fashioned, low-browed, thatch-covered stone cottage, with a rude portico of rustic woodwork overrun with jasmine and virgin-bower, and a pretty flower garden sloping down in successive terraces to the edge of the basin. Beside this, there was no other house in sight, unless it were part of the roof of a mill which stood in the low ground on the brink of the second fall, surrounded with a mass of willows. But the tall steeple of a country church, raising itself heavenward above the brow of the hill, seemed to show that, although concealed by the undulations of the ground, a village was hard at hand.

The morning had changed a second time, a hazy film had crept up to the zenith, and the sun was now covered with a pale golden veil, and a slight current of air down the gorge ruffled the water.

It was a capital pool, famous for being the temporary haunt of the very finest fish, which were wont to lie there awhile, as if to recruit themselves after the exertions of leaping the two falls and stemming the double rapid, before attempting to ascend the stream farther.

Few, however, even of the best and boldest fishermen, cared to wet a line in its waters, in consequence of the supposed impossibility of following a heavy fish through the gorge below, or checking him at the brink of the fall. It is true, that throughout the length of the pass, the current was broken by bare, slippery rocks peering above the waters, at intervals, which might be cleared by an active cragsman; and it had been in fact reconnoitred by Jasper and others in cool blood, but the result of the examination was that it was deemed impassable.

Thinking, however, little of striking a large fish, and perhaps desiring to waste a little time before scaling the banks and emerging on the high-road, Jasper threw a favorite fly of peacock's herl and gold tinsel lightly across the water; and, almost before he had time to think, had hooked a monstrous fish, which, at the very first leap, he set down as weighing at least thirty pounds.

Thereupon followed a splendid display of piscatory skill. Well knowing that his fish must be lost if he once should succeed in getting his head down the rapid, Jasper exerted every nerve, and exhausted every art to humor, to meet, to restrain, to check him. Four times the fish rushed for the pass, and four times Jasper met him so stoutly with the butt, trying his tackle to the very utmost, that he succeeded in forcing him from the perilous spot. Round and round the pool he had piloted him, and had taken post at length, hoping that the worst was already over, close to the opening of the rocky chasm.

And now perhaps waxing too confident, he checked his fish too sharply. Stung into fury, the monster sprang five times in succession into the air, lashing the water with his angry tail, and then rushed like an arrow down the chasm.

He was gone—but Jasper's blood was up, and thinking of nothing but his sport, he dashed forward, and embarked, with a fearless foot, into the terrible descent.

Leap after leap he took with beautiful precision, alighting firm and erect on the centre of each slippery block, and bounding thence to the next with unerring instinct, guiding his fish the while with consummate skill through the intricacies of the pass.

There were now but three more leaps to be taken before he would reach the flat table-rock above the fall, which once attained, he would have firm foothold and a fair field; already he rejoiced, triumphant in the success of his bold attainment, and confident in victory, when a shrill female shriek reached his ears from the pretty flower-garden; caught by the sound, he diverted his eyes, just as he leaped, toward the place whence it came; his foot slipped, and the next instant he was flat on his back in the swifter stream, where it shot the most furiously over the glassy rock. He struggled manfully, but in vain. The smooth, slippery surface afforded no purchase to his gripping fingers, no hold to his laboring feet. One fearful, agonizing conflict with the wild waters, and he was swept helplessly over the edge of the fall, his head, as he glanced down foot foremost, striking the rocky brink with fearful violence.

He was plunged into the deep pool, and whirled round and round by the dark eddies long before he rose, but still, though stunned and half-disabled, he strove terribly to support himself, but it was all in vain.

Again he sunk and rose once more, and as he rose that wild shriek again reached his ears, and his last glance fell upon a female form wringing her hands in despair on the bank, and a young man rushing down in wild haste from the cottage on the hill.

He felt that aid was at hand, and struck out again for life—for dear life!

But the water seemed to fail beneath him.

A slight flash sprang across his eyes, his brain reeled, and all was blackness.

He sunk to the bottom, spurned it with his feet, and rose once more, but not to the surface.

His quivering blue hands emerged alone above the relentless waters, grasped for a little moment at empty space, and then disappeared.

The circling ripples closed over him, and subsided into stillness.

He felt, knew, suffered nothing more.

His young, warm heart was cold and lifeless—his soul had lost its consciousness—the vital spark had faded into darkness—perhaps was quenched for ever.

A Gallant Poacher

John Buchan

WHEN THE HISPANA CROSSED THE BRIDGE OF LARRIG, HIS
Majesty's late Attorney-General was modestly concealed in a
bush of broom on the Crask side, from which he could watch
the sullen stretches of the Lang Whang. He was carefully
dressed for the part in a pair of Wattie Lithgow's old trousers
much too short for him, a waistcoat and jacket which belonged
to Sime the butler and which had been made about the year
1890, and a vulgar flannel shirt borrowed from Shapp. He was
innocent of a collar, he had not shaved for two days, and as
he had forgotten to have his hair cut before leaving London
his locks were of a disreputable length. Last, he had a shocking old hat of Sir Archie's from which the lining had long
since gone. His hands were sunburnt and grubby, and he had
removed his signet-ring. A light ten-foot greenheart rod lay
beside him, already put up, and to the tapered line was fixed a
tapered cast ending in a strange little cocked fly. As he waited,
he was busy oiling fly and line.

His glass showed him an empty haugh, save for the figure of Jimsie at the far end close to the Wood of Larrigmore.

The sun-warmed waters of the river drowsed in the long dead stretches, curled at rare intervals by the faintest western breeze. The banks were crisp green turf, scarcely broken by a boulder, but five yards from them the moss began—a wilderness of hags and tussocks. Somewhere in its depths he knew that Benjie lay coiled like an adder, waiting on events.

Leithen's plan, like all great strategy, was simple. Everything depended on having Jimsie out of sight of the Lang Whang for half an hour. Given that, he believed he might kill a salmon. He had marked out a pool where in the evening fish were usually stirring, one of those irrational haunts which no piscatorial psychologist has ever explained. If he could fish fine and far, he might cover it from a spot below a high bank where only the top of his rod would be visible to watchers at a distance. Unfortunately, that spot was on the other side of the stream. With such tackle, landing a salmon would be a critical business, but there was one chance in ten that it might be accomplished; Benjie would be at hand to conceal the fish, and he himself would disappear silently into the Crask thickets. But every step bristled with horrid dangers. Jimsie might be faithful to his post—in which case it was hopeless; he might find the salmon dour, or a fish might break him in the landing, or Jimsie might return to find him brazenly tethered to forbidden game. It was no good thinking about it. On one thing he was decided; if he were caught, he would not try to escape. That would mean retreat in the direction of Crask, and an exploration of the Crask covers would assuredly reveal what must at all costs be concealed. No. He would go quietly into captivity, and trust to his base appearance to let off with a drubbing.

As he waited, watching the pools turn from gold to bronze, as the sun sank behind the Glenraden peaks, he suffered the inevitable reaction. The absurdities seemed huge as mountains, the difficulties innumerable as the waves of the sea. There remained less than an hour in which there would be sufficient light to fish—Jimsie was immovable (he had just lit his pipe and was sitting in meditation on a big stone)—every moment the Larrig waters were cooling with the chill of evening. Leithen consulted his watch, and found it half-past eight. He had lost his wrist-watch, and had brought his hunter, attached to a thin gold chain. That was foolish, so he slipped the chain from his buttonhole and drew it through the arm-hole of his waistcoat.

Suddenly he rose to his feet, for things were happening at the far end of the haugh. Jimsie stood in an attitude of expectation—he seemed to be hearing something far up-stream. Leithen heard it too, the cry of excited men . . . Jimsie stood on one foot for a moment in doubt, then he turned and doubled toward the Wood of Larrigmore. . . . The gallant Crossby had got to business and was playing hare to the hounds inside the park wall. If human nature had not changed, Leithen thought, the whole force would presently join in the chase—Angus and Lennox and Jimsie and Davie and doubtless many volunteers. Heaven send fleetness and wind to the South London Harrier, for it was his duty to occupy the interest of every male in

Strathlarrig till such time as he subsided with angry expostulations in captivity.

The road was empty, the valley was deserted, when Leithen raced across the bridge and up the south side of the river. It was not two hundred yards to his chosen stand, a spit of gravel below a high bank at the tail of a long pool. Close to the other bank, nearly thirty yards off, was the shelf where fish lay of an evening. He tested the water with his hand, and its temperature was at least sixty degrees. His theory, which he had learned long ago from the aged Bostonian, was that under such conditions some subconscious memory revived in salmon of their early days as parr when they fed on surface insects, and that they could be made to take a dry fly.

He got out his line to the required length with half a dozen casts in the air, and then put his fly three feet above the spot where a salmon was wont to lie. It was a curious type of cast, which he had been practising lately in the early morning, for by an adroit check he made the fly alight in a curl, so that it floated for a second or two with the leader in a straight line away from it. In this way he believed that the most suspicious fish would see nothing to alarm him, nothing but a hapless insect derelict on the water.

Sir Archie had spoken truth in describing Leithen to Wattie Lithgow as an artist. His long, straight, delicate casts were art indeed. Like thistledown the fly dropped, like thistledown it floated over the head of the salmon, but like thistledown it was disregarded. There was, indeed, a faint stirring of curiosity.

From where he stood Leithen could see that slight ruffling of the surface which means an observant fish. . . .

Already ten minutes had been spent in this barren art. The crisis craved other measures.

His new policy meant a short line, so with infinite stealth and care Leithen waded up the side of the water, sometimes treading precarious ledges of peat, sometimes waist-deep in mud and pond-weed, till he was within twenty feet of the fishing-ground. Here he had not the high bank for a shelter, and would have been sadly conspicuous to Jimsie, had that sentinel remained at his post. He crouched low and cast as before with the same curl just ahead of the chosen spot.

But now his tactics were different. So soon as the fly had floated past where he believed the fish to be, he sank it by a dexterous twist of the rod-point, possible only with a short line. The fly was no longer a winged thing; drawn away under water, it roused in the salmon early memories of succulent nymphs.

. . . At the first cast there was a slight swirl which meant that a fish near the surface had turned to follow the lure. The second cast the line straightened and moved swiftly up-stream.

Leithen had killed in his day many hundreds of salmon— once in Norway a notable beast of fifty-five pounds. But no salmon he had ever hooked had stirred in his breast such excitement as this modest fellow of eight pounds. "'Tis not so wide as a church-door," he reflected with Mercutio, "but 'twill suffice"—if I can only land him. But a dry-fly cast and a ten-foot rod are a frail wherewithal for killing a fish against time. With his ordinary fifteen-footer and gut of moderate strength he could have brought the little salmon to grass in five minutes, but now there was immense risk of a break, and a break would mean that the whole enterprise had failed. He dared not exert pressure; on the other hand, he could not follow the fish except by making himself conspicuous on the greensward. Worst of all, he had at the best ten minutes for the job.

Thirty yards off, an otter slid into the water. Leithen wished he was King of the Otters, as in the Highland tale, to summon the brute to his aid.

The ten minutes had lengthened to fifteen—nine hundred seconds of heart disease—when, wet to the waist, he got his pocket gaff into the salmon's side and drew it on to the spit of gravel where he had started fishing. A dozen times he thought he had lost, and once when the fish ran straight up the pool his line was carried out to its last yard of backing. He gave thanks to high Heaven, when, as he landed it, he observed that the fly had all but lost its hold and in another minute would have been freed. By such narrow margins are great deeds accomplished.

He snapped the cast from the line and buried it in mud. Then cautiously he raised his head above the high bank. The gloaming was gathering fast, and so far as he could see the haugh was still empty. Pushing his rod along the ground he scrambled on to the turf.

Then he had a grievous shock. Jimsie had reappeared, and he was in full view of him. Moreover, there were two men on bicycles coming up the road, who, with the deplorable instinct of human nature, would be certain to join in any pursuit. He was on turf as short as a lawn, cumbered with a telltale rod and a poached salmon. The friendly hags were a dozen yards off, and before he could reach them his damning baggage would be noted.

At this supreme moment he had an inspiration, derived from the memory of the otter. To get out his knife, cut a ragged wedge from the fish, and roll it in his handkerchief was the work of three seconds. To tilt the rod over the bank so that it lay in the deep shadow was the work of three more. . . . Jimsie had seen him, for a wild cry came down the stream, a cry which brought the cyclists off their machines and set them staring in his direction. Leithen dropped his gaff after the rod, and began running towards the Larrig Bridge—slowly, limpingly, like a frightened man with no resolute purpose of escape. And as he ran he prayed that Benjie from the deeps of the moss had seen what had been done and drawn the proper inference.

It was a bold bluff, for he had decided to make the salmon evidence for, not against, him. He hobbled down the bank, looking over his shoulder often as if in terror, and almost ran into the arms of the cyclists, who, warned by Jimsie's yells, were waiting to intercept him. He dodged them, however, and cut across to the road, for he had seen that Jimsie had paused and had noted the salmon lying blatantly on the sward, a silver splash in the twilight. Leithen doubled up the road as if going towards Strathlarrig, and Jimsie, the fleet of foot, did not catch up with him till almost on the edge of the Wood of Larrigmore. The cyclists, who had remounted, arrived at the same moment to find a wretched muddy tramp in the grip of a stalwart but breathless gillie.

"I tell ye I was daein' nae harm," the tramp whined. "I was walkin' up the waterside—there's nae law to keep a body frae walkin' up a waterside when there's nae fence—and I seen an auld otter killin' a saumon. The fish is there still to prove I'm no leein'."

"There is a fush, but you was thinkin' to steal the fush, and you would have had it in your breeks if I hadna seen you. That is poachn', ma man, and you will come up to Strathlarrig. The master said that any one goin' near the watter was to be lockit up, and you will be lockit up. You can tell all the lees you like in the mornin'."

Then a thought struck Jimsie. He wanted the salmon, for the subject of otters in the Larrig had long been a matter of dispute between him and Angus, and here was evidence for his own view.

"Would you two gentlemen oblige me by watchin' this man while I rin back and get the fush? Bash him on the head if he offers to rin."

The cyclists, who were journalists out to enjoy the evening air, willingly agreed, but Leithen showed no wish to escape. He begged a fag in a beggar's whine, and since he seemed peaceable, the two kept a good distance for fear of infection. He stood making damp streaks in the dusty road, a pitiable specimen of humanity, for his original get-up was not improved by the liquefaction of his clothes and a generous legacy of slimy peat. He seemed to be nervous, which, indeed, he was, for if Benjie had not seized his chance he was utterly done, and if Jimsie should light upon his rod he was gravely compromised.

But when Jimsie returned in a matter of ten minutes it was empty-handed.

"I never kenned the like," he proclaimed. "That otter has come back and gotten the fush. Ach, the maleecious brute!"

The rest of Leithen's progress was not triumphant. He was conducted to the Strathlarrig lodge, where Angus, whose temper and wind had alike been ruined by the pursuit of Crossby, laid savage hands upon him, and frog-marched him to the back premises. The head keeper scarcely heeded Jimsie's tale. "Ach, ye poachin' va-aga-bond. It is the jyle ye'll get," he roared, for Angus was in a mood which could only be relieved by violence of speech and action. Rumbling Gaelic imprecations, he hustled his prisoner into an outhouse, which had once been a larder and was now a supplementary garage, slammed and locked the door, and, as a final warning, kicked it viciously with his foot, as if to signify what awaited the culprit when the time came to sit on his case.

Early next morning, when the great door of Strathlarrig House was opened and the maids had begun their work, Oliphant, the butler—a stately man who had been trained in a ducal family—crossed the hall to reconnoitre the outer world.

There he found an under-housemaid, nursing a strange package which she averred she had found on the doorstep. It was some two feet long, swathed in brown paper, and attached to its string was a letter inscribed to Mr. Junius Bandicott.

The parcel was clammy and Oliphant handled it gingerly. He cut the cord, disentangled the letter, and revealed an oblong of green rushes bound with string. The wrapping must have been insecure, for something forthwith slipped from the rushes and flopped on the marble floor, revealing to Oliphant's disgusted eyes a small salmon, blue and stiff in death.

At that moment Junius, always an early bird, came whistling downstairs. So completely was he convinced of the inviolability of the Strathlarrig waters that the spectacle caused him no foreboding.

"What are you flinging fish about for, Oliphant?" he asked cheerfully.

The butler presented him with the envelope. He opened it and extracted a dirty half-sheet of notepaper, on which was printed in capitals, "With the compliments of John Macnab."

Amazement, chagrin, amusement followed each other on Junius's open countenance. Then he picked up the fish and marched out of doors shouting "Angus" at the top of a notably powerful voice. The sound brought the scared face of Professor Babwater to his bedroom window.

Angus, who had been up since four, appeared from Lady Maisie's pool where he had been contemplating the waters.

His vigil had not improved his appearance or his temper, for his eye was red and choleric and his beard was wild as a mountain goat's. He cast one look at the salmon, surmised the truth, and held up imploring hands to Heaven.

"John Macnab!" said Junius sternly. "What have you got to say to that?"

Angus had nothing audible to say. He was handling the fish with feverish hands and peering at its jaws, and presently under his fingers a segment fell out.

"That fush was cleekit," observed Lennox, who had come up. "It was never catched with a flee."

"Ye're a leear," Angus roared. "Just tak a look at the mouth of it. There's the mark of the huke, ye gommeril. The fush was took wi' a rod and line."

"You may reckon it was," observed Junius. "I trust John Macnab to abide by the rules of the game."

Suddenly light seemed to break in on Angus's soul. He bellowed for Jimsie, who was placidly making his way towards the group at the door, lighting his pipe as he went.

"Look at that, James Mackenzie. Ay, look at it. Feast your een on it. You wass tellin' me there wass otters in the Largg and I said there wass not. You wass tellin' me there wass an otter had a fush last night at the Lang Whang. There's your otter and be damned to ye!"

Jimsie, slow of comprehension, rubbed his eyes. "Where wass you findin' the fush? Ay, it's the one I seen last night. That otter must be wrang in the heid."

"It's not wrang in the heid. It's you that are wrang in the heid, James Mackenzie. The otter is a ver-ra clever man, and its name will be John Macnab."

Slowly enlightenment dawned on Jimsie's mind.

"He was the tramp," he ingeminated. "He was the tramp."

"And he's still lockit up," Angus cried joyfully. "Wait till I get my hands on him." He was striding off for the garage when a word from Junius held him back.

"You won't find him there. I gave orders last night to let him go. You know, Angus, you told me he was only a tramp that had been seen walking up the river."

"We will catch him yet!" cried the vindictive head keeper. "Get you on your bicycle, Jimsie, and away after him. He'll be on the Muirtown road—There's just the one road he can travel."

"No, you don't," said Junius. "I don't want him here. He had beaten us fairly in a match of wits, and the business is finished."

"But the thing's no' possible," Jimsie moaned. "The skeeliest fisher would not take a saumon in the Lang Whang with a flee. . . . And I wasna away many meenutes. . . . And the tramp was a poor shilpit body—not like a fisher or any kind of gentleman at all—at all. . . . And he hadna a rod. . . . The thing's no' possible."

"I think it was the Deevil."

Fish Are Such Liars

Roland Pertwee

THERE HAD BEEN A FUSS IN THE POOL BENEATH THE ALDERS, and the small rainbow trout, with a skitter of his tail, flashed upstream, a hurt and angry fish. For three consecutive mornings he had taken the rise in that pool, and it injured his pride to be jostled from his drift just when the May fly was coming up in numbers. If his opponent had been a half-pounder like himself, he would have stayed and fought, but when an old hen fish, weighing fully three pounds, with a mouth like a rat hole and a carnivorous, cannibalistic eye rises from the reed beds and occupies the place, flight is the only effective argument.

But Rainbow was very much provoked. He had chosen his place with care. Now the May fly was up, the little French chalk stream was full of rising fish, and he knew by experience that strangers are unpopular in that season. To do one's self justice during a hatch, one must find a place where the fly drifts nicely overhead with the run of the stream, and natural drifts are scarce even in a chalk stream. He was not content to leap at the fly like a hysterical youngster who measured his weight in ounces and his wits in milligrams. He had reached that time of life which demanded that he should feed off the surface by suction rather than exertion. No living thing is more particular about his table manners than a trout, and Rainbow was no exception.

"It's a sickening thing," he said to himself, "and a hard shame." He added: "Get out of my way," to a couple of fat young chub with negroid mouths who were bubbling the surface in the silly, senseless fashion of their kind.

"Chub indeed!"

But even the chub had a home and he had none—and the life of a homeless river dweller is precarious.

"I will not and shall not be forced back to midstream," he said.

For, save at eventide or in very special circumstances, trout of personality do not frequent open water where they must compete for every insect with the wind, the lightning-swift sweep of swallows and martins, and even the laborious pursuit of predatory dragon-flies with their bronze wings and bodies like rods of colored glass. Even as he spoke he saw a three-ounce leap at a dapping May fly which was scooped out of his jaws by a passing swallow. Rainbow heard the tiny click as the May fly's body cracked against the bird's beak. A single wing of yellowy gossamer floated downward and settled upon the water. Under the shelving banks to right and left, where the fly, discarding its nymph and still too damp for its virgin flight, drifted downstream, a dozen heavy trout were feeding thoughtfully and selectively.

"If only some angler would catch one of them, I might slip in and occupy the place before it gets known there's a vacancy."

But this uncharitable hope was not fulfilled, and with another whisk of his tail he propelled himself into the unknown waters upstream. A couple of strands of rusty barbed wire, relic of the war, spanned the shallows from bank to bank. Passing beneath them he came to a narrow reach shaded by willows, to the first of which was nailed a board bearing the words Pêche Réservée. He had passed out of the communal into private water—water running languidly over manes of emerald weed between clumps of alder, willow herb, tall crimson sorrel and masses of yellow iris. Ahead, like an apple-green rampart, rose the wooded heights of a forest; on either side were flat mead-ows of yellowing hay. Overhead, the vast expanse of blue June sky was tufted with rambling clouds. "My scales!" said Rain-bow. "Here's water!"'

But it was vain to expect any of the best places in such a reach would be vacant, and to avoid a recurrence of his unhappy encounter earlier in the morning, Rainbow contin-ued his journey until he came to a spot where the river took one of those unaccountable right-angle bends which result in a pool, shallow on the one side, but slanting into deeps on the other. Above it was a water break, a swirl, smoothing, as it reached the pool, into a sleek, swift run, with an eddy which bore all the lighter floating things of the river over the calm surface of the little backwater, sheltered from above by a high shelving bank and a tangle of bramble and herb. Here in this backwater the twig, the broken reed, the leaf, the cork, the fly floated in suspended activity for a few instants until drawn back by invisible magnetism to the main current.

Rainbow paused in admiration. At the tail of the pool two sound fish were rising with regularity, but in the backwater beyond the eddy the surface was still and unbroken. Watching open-eyed, Rainbow saw not one but a dozen May flies, fat, juicy, and damp from the nymph, drift in, pause, and carried away untouched. It was beyond the bounds of possibility that such a place could be vacant, but there was the evidence of his eyes to prove it; and nothing if not a tryer, Rainbow darted across the stream and parked himself six inches below the water to await events.

It so happened that at the time of his arrival the hatch of fly was temporarily suspended, which gave Rainbow leisure to make a survey of his new abode. Beyond the eddy was a submerged snag—the branch of an apple tree borne there by heavy rains, water-logged, anchored, and intricate—an excellent place to break an angler's line. The river bank on his right was riddled under water with old rat holes, than which there is no better sanctuary. Below him and to the left was a dense bed of weeds brushed flat by the flow of the stream.

"If it comes to the worst," said Rainbow, "a smart fish could do a get-away here with very little ingenuity, even from a cannibalistic old hen like—hullo!"

The exclamation was excited by the apparition of a gauzy shadow on the water, which is what a May fly seen from below

214

looks like. Resisting a vulgar inclination to leap at it with the violence of a youngster, Rainbow backed into the correct position which would allow the stream to present the morsel, so to speak, upon a tray. Which it did—and scarcely a dimple on the surface to tell what had happened.

"Very nicely taken, if you will accept the praise of a complete stranger," said a low, soft voice, one inch behind his line of sight.

Without turning to see by whom he had been addressed, Rainbow flicked a yard upstream and came back with the current four feet away. In the spot he had occupied an instant before lay a great old trout of the most benign aspect, who could not have weighed less than four pounds.

"I beg your pardon," said Rainbow, "but I had no idea that any one—that is, I just dropped in *en passant,* and finding an empty house, I made so bold—"

"There is no occasion to apologize," said Old Trout seductively. "I did not come up from the bottom as early to-day as is my usual habit at this season. Yesterday's hatch was singularly bountiful and it is possible I did myself too liberally."

"Yes, but a gentleman of your weight and seniority can hardly fail to be offended at finding—"

"Not at all," Old Trout broke in. "I perceive you are a well-conducted fish who does not advertise his appetite in a loud and splashing fashion."

Overcome by the charm of Old Trout's manner and address, Rainbow reduced the distance separating them to a matter of inches.

"Then you do not want me to go?" he asked.

"On the contrary, dear young sir, stay by all means and take the rise. You are, I perceive, of the rainbow or, as they say here in France, of the Arc-en-ciel family. As a youngster I had the impression that I should turn out a rainbow, but events proved it was no more than the bloom, the natural sheen of youth."

"To speak the truth, sir," said Rainbow, "unless you had told me to the contrary, I would surely have thought you one of us."

Old Trout shook his tail. "You are wrong," he said. "I am from Dulverton, an English trout farm on the Exe, of which you will have heard. You are doubtless surprised to find an English fish in French waters."

"I am indeed," Rainbow replied, sucking in a passing May fly with such excellent good manners that it was hard to believe he was feeding. "Then you, sir," he added, "must know all about the habits of men."

"I may justly admit that I do," Old Trout agreed. "Apart from being hand-reared, have in my twelve years of life studied the species in moods of activity, passivity, duplicity, and violence."

Rainbow remarked that such must doubtless have proved of invaluable service. It did not, however, explain the mystery of his presence on a French river.

"For, sir," he added, "Dulverton, as once I heard when enjoying 'A Chat about Rivers,' delivered by a much-traveled sea trout, is situated in the west of England, and without crossing the Channel I am unable to explain how you arrived here. Had you belonged to the salmon family, with which, sir, it is evident you have no connection, the explanation would be simple, but in the circumstances it baffles my understanding."

Old Trout waved one of his fins airily. "Yet cross the Channel I certainly did," said he, "and at a period in history which I venture to state will not readily be forgotten. It was during the war, my dear young friend, and I was brought in a can, in company with a hundred yearlings, to this river, or rather the upper reaches of this river, by a young officer who wished to further an entente between English and French fish even as the war was doing with the mankind of these two nations."

Old Trout sighed a couple of bubbles and arched his body this way and that.

"There was a gentleman and a sportsman," he said. "A man who was acquainted with our people as I dare to say very few are acquainted. Had it ever been my lot to fall victim to a lover of the rod, I could have done so without regret to his. If you will take a look at my tail, you will observe that the letter W is perforated on the upper side. He presented me with this distinguishing mark before committing me, with his blessing, to the water."

"I have seldom seen a tail more becomingly decorated," said Rainbow. "But what happened to your benefactor?"

Old Trout's expression became infinitely sad. "If I could answer that," said he, "I were indeed a happy trout. For many weeks after he put me into the river I used to watch him in what little spare time he was able to obtain, casting a dry fly with the exquisite precision and likeness to nature in all the likely pools and runs and eddies near his battery position. Oh, minnows! It was a pleasure to watch that man, even as it was his pleasure to watch us. His bravery too! I call to mind a dozen times when he fished unmoved and unstartled while bullets from machine guns were pecking at the water like herons and thudding into the mud banks upon which he stood."

"An angler!" remarked Rainbow. "It would be no lie to say I like him the less on that account."

Old Trout became unexpectedly stern.

"Why so?" he retorted severely. "Have I not said he was also a gentleman and a sportsman? My officer was neither a pot-hunter nor a beast of prey. He was a purist—a man who took delight in pitting his knowledge of nature against the subtlest and most suspicious intellectual forces of the wild. Are you so young as not yet to have learned the exquisite enjoyment of escaping disaster and avoiding error by the exercise of personal ingenuity? Pray, do not reply, for I would hate to think so hard a thing of any trout. We as a race exist by virtue of our brilliant intellectuality and hypersensitive selectivity. In waters where there are no pike and only an occasional otter, but for the machinations of men, where should we turn to school our wits? Danger is our mainstay, for I tell you, Rainbow, that trout are composed of two senses—appetite, which makes of us fools, and suspicion, which teaches us to be wise."

Greatly chastened not alone by what Old Trout had said but by the forensic quality of his speech, Rainbow rose short and put a promising May fly onto the wing.

"I am glad to observe," said Old Trout, "that you are not without conscience."

"To tell the truth, sir," Rainbow replied apologetically, "my nerve this morning has been rudely shaken, but for which I should not have shown such want of good sportsmanship."

And with becoming brevity he told the tale of his eviction from the pool downstream. Old Trout listened gravely, only once moving, and that to absorb a small blue dun, an insect which he keenly relished.

"A regrettable affair," he admitted, "but as I have often observed, women, who are the gentlest creatures under water in adversity, are a thought lacking in moderation in times of abundance. They are apt to snatch."

"But for a turn of speed, she would certainly have snatched me," said Rainbow.

"Very shocking," said Old Trout. "Cannibals are disgusting. They destroy the social amenities of the river. We fish have but little family life and should therefore aim to cultivate a freemasonry of good-fellowship among ourselves. For my part, I am happy to line up with other well-conducted trout and content myself with what happens along with my own particular drift. Pardon me!" he added, breasting Rainbow to one side. "I invited you to take the rise of May fly, but I must ask you to leave the duns alone." Then, fearing this remark might be construed to reflect adversely upon his hospitality, he proceeded: "I have a reason which I will explain later. For the moment we are discussing the circumstances that led to my presence in this river."

"To be sure—your officer. He never succeeded in deluding you with his skill?"

"That would have been impossible," said Old Trout, "for I had taken up a position under the far bank where he could only have reached me with a fly by wading in a part of the river which was in view of a German sniper."

"Wily!" Rainbow chuckled. "Cunning work, sir."

"Perhaps," Old Trout admitted, "although I have since reproached myself with cowardice. However, I was at the time a very small fish and a certain amount of nervousness is forgivable in the young."

At this gracious acknowledgment the rose-colored hue in Rainbow's rainbow increased noticeably—in short, he blushed.

"From where I lay," Old Trout went on, "I was able to observe the maneuvers of my officer and greatly profit thereby."

"But excuse me, sir," said Rainbow, "I have heard it said that an angler of the first class is invisible from the river."

"He is invisible to the fish he is trying to catch," Old Trout admitted, "but it must be obvious that he is not invisible to the fish who lie beside or below him. I would also remind you that during the war every tree, every scrap of vegetation, and every vestige of natural cover had been torn up, trampled down, razed. The river banks were as smooth as the top of your head.

Even the buttercup, that very humorous flower that tangles up the bark cast of so many industrious anglers, was absent. Those who fished on the Western Front had little help from nature."

Young Rainbow sighed, for, only a few days before, his tongue had been badly scratched by an artificial alder which had every appearance of reality.

"It would seem," he said, "that this war had its merits."

"My young friend," said Old Trout, "you never made a greater mistake. A desire on the part of our soldiery to vary a monotonous diet of bully beef and biscuit often drove them to resort to villainous methods of assault against our kind."

"Nets?" gasped Rainbow in horror.

"Worse than nets—bombs," Old Trout replied. "A small oval black thing called a Mills bomb, which the shameless fellows flung into deep pools."

"But surely the chances of being hit by such a—"

"You reveal a pathetic ignorance," said Old Trout. "There is no question of being hit. The wretched machine exploded under water and burst our people's insides or stunned us so that we floated dead to the surface. I well remember my officer coming upon such a group of marauders one evening—yes, and laying about him with his fists in defiance of King's Regulations and the Manual of Military Law. Two of them he seized by the collar and the pants and flung into the river. Spinning minnows, that was a sight worth seeing! 'You low swine,' I heard him say; 'you trash, you muck! Isn't there enough carnage without this sort of thing?' Afterward he sat on the bank

with the two dripping men and talked to them for their souls'
sake.

" 'Look ahead, boys. Ask yourselves what are we fighting
for? Decent homes to live in at peace with one another, fields
to till and forests and rivers to give us a day's sport and fun.
It's our rotten job to massacre each other, but, by gosh, don't
let's massacre the harmless rest of nature as well. At least, let's
give 'em a running chance. Boys, in the years ahead, when all
the mess is cleared up, I look forward to coming back to this
old spot, when there is alder growing by the banks, and willow herb and tall reeds and the drone of insects instead of the
rumble of those guns. I don't want to come back to a dead river
that I helped to kill, but to a river ringed with rising fish—
some of whom were old comrades of the war.' He went on to
tell of us hundred Dulverton trout that he had marked with
the letter W. 'Give 'em their chance,' he said, 'and in the years
to come those beggars will reward us a hundred times over.
They'll give us a finer thrill and put up a cleaner fight than old
Jerry ever contrived.' Those were emotional times, and though
you may be reluctant to believe me, one of those two very wet
men dripped water from his eyes as well as his clothing.

"'Many's the 'appy afternoon I've 'ad with a roach pole
on Brentford Canal,' he sniffed, 'though I've never yet tried
m' hand against a trout.' 'You shall do it now,' said my officer,
and during the half-hour that was left of daylight that dripping soldier had his first lesson in the most delicate art in the
world. I can see them now—the clumsy, wet fellow and my

officer timing him, timing him—'one and two, and one and two, and—' The action of my officer's wrist with its persuasive flick was the prettiest thing I have ever seen."

"Did he carry out his intention and come back after the war?" Rainbow asked.

"I shall never know," Old Trout replied. "I do not even know if he survived it. There was a great battle—a German drive. For hours they shelled the river front, and many falling short exploded in our midst with terrible results. My own bank was torn to shreds and our people suffered. How they suffered! About noon the infantry came over—hordes in field gray. There wire pontoons, rope bridges and hand-to-hand fights on both banks and even in the stream itself."

"And your officer?"

"I saw him once, before the water was stamped dense into liquid mud and dyed by the blood of men. He was in the thick of it, unarmed, and a German officer called on him to surrender. For answer he struck him in the face with a light cane. Ah, that wrist action! Then a shell burst, smothering the water with clods of fallen earth and other things."

"Then you never knew?"

"I never knew, although that night I searched among the dead. Next day I went downstream, for the water in that place was polluted with death. The bottom of the pool in which I had my place was choked with strange and mangled tenants that were not good to look upon. We trout are a clean people that will not readily abide in dirty houses. I am a Dulverton trout, where the water is filtered by the hills and runs cool over stones."

"And you have stayed here ever since?"

Old Trout shrugged a fin. "I have moved with the times. Choosing a place according to the needs of my weight."

"And you have never been caught, sir, by any other angler?"

"Am I not here?" Old Trout answered with dignity.

"Oh, quite, sir. I had only thought, perhaps, as a younger fish enthusiasm might have resulted to your disadvantage, but that, nevertheless, you had been returned."

"Returned! Returned!" echoed Old Trout. "Returned to the frying-pan! Where on earth did you pick up that expression? We are in France, my young friend; we are not on the Test, the Itchen, or the Kennet. In this country it is not the practice of anglers to return anything, however miserable in size."

"But nowadays," Rainbow protested, "there are Englishmen and Americans on the river who show us more consideration."

"They may show you consideration," said Old Trout, "but I am of an importance that neither asks for nor expects it. Oblige me by being a little more discreet with your plurals. In the impossible event of my being deceived and caught, I should be introduced to a glass case with an appropriate background of rocks and reeds."

"But, sir, with respect, how can you be so confident of your unassailabilty?" Rainbow demanded, edging into position to accept an attractive May fly with yellow wings that was drifting downstream toward him.

"How?" Old Trout responded. "Because—" Then suddenly: "Leave it, you fool!"

Rainbow had just broken the surface when the warning came. The yellow-winged May fly was wrenched off the water with a wet squeak. A tangle of limp cast lapped itself round the upper branches of a willow far upstream and a raw voice exclaimed something venomous in French. By common consent the two fish went down.

"Well, really," expostulated Old Trout, "I hoped you were above that kind of thing! Nearly to fall victim to a downstream angler. It's a little too much! And think of the effect it will have on my prestige. Why, that incompetent fool will go about boasting that he rose me. Me!"

For some minutes Rainbow was too crestfallen even to apologize. At last: "I am afraid," he said, "I was paying more heed to what you were saying than to my own conduct. I never expected to be fished from above. The fly was an uncommonly good imitation and it is a rare thing for a Frenchman to use Four-X gut."

"Rubbish," said Old Trout testily. "These are mere half-pound arguments. Four-X gut, when associated with a fourteen-stone shadow, should deceive nothing over two ounces. I saved your life, but it is all very provoking. If that is a sample of your general demeanor, it is improbable that you will ever reach a pound."

"At this season we are apt to be careless," Rainbow wailed. "And nowadays it is so hard, sir, to distinguish the artificial fly from the real."

"No one expects you to do so," was the answer, "but common prudence demands that you should pay some attention to the manner in which it is presented. A May fly does not hit the water with a splash, neither is it able to sustain itself in midstream against the current. Have you ever seen a natural insect leave a broadening wake of cutwater behind its tail? Never mind the fly, my dear boy, but watch the manner of its presentation. Failure to do that has cost many of our people their lives."

"You speak," said Rainbow, a shade sulkily, "as though it were a disgrace for a trout ever to suffer defeat at the hands of an angler."

"Which indeed it is, save in exceptional circumstances," Old Trout answered. "I do not say that a perfect upstream cast from a well-concealed angler, when the fly alights dry and cocked and dances at even speed with the current, may not deceive us to our fall. And I would be the last to say that a grasshopper skillfully dapped on the surface through the branches of an overhanging tree will not inevitably bring about our destruction. But I do most emphatically say that in such a spot as this, where the slightest defect in presentation is multiplied a hundred-fold by the varying water speeds, a careless rise is unpardonable. There is only one spot—and that a matter of twelve yards downstream—from which a fly can be drifted over me with any semblance to nature. Even so, there is not one angler in a thousand who can make that cast with success, by reason of a willow which cramps the back cast and the manner in which these alders on our left sprawl across the pool."

Rainbow did not turn about to verify these statements because it is bad form for a trout to face downstream. He contented himself by replying, with a touch of acerbity: "I should have thought, sir, with the feelings you expressed regarding sportsmanship, you would have found such a sanctuary too dull for your entertainment."

"Every remark you make serves to aggravate the impression of your ignorance," Old Trout replied. "Would you expect a trout of my intelligence to put myself in some place where I am exposed to the vulgar assaults·of every amateur upon the bank? Of the green boy who lashes the water into foam, of the purblind peasant who slings his fly at me with a clod of earth or a tail of weed attached to the hook? In this place I invite attention from none but the best people—the expert, the purist."

"I understood you to say that there were none such in these parts," grumbled Rainbow.

"There are none who have succeeded in deceiving me," was the answer. "As a fact, for the last few days I have been vastly entranced by an angler who, by any standard is deserving of praise. His presentation is flawless and the only fault I can detect in him is a tendency to overlook piscine psychology. He will be with us in a few minutes, since he knows it is my habit to lunch at noon."

"Pardon the interruption," said Rainbow, "but there is a gallant hatch of fly going down. I can hear your two neighbors at the tail of the pool rising steadily."

Old Trout assumed an indulgent air. "We will go up if you wish," said he, "but you will be well advised to observe my counsel before taking the rise, because if my angler keeps his appointment you will most assuredly be *meunière* before nightfall."

At this unpleasant prophecy Rainbow shivered. "Let us keep to weed," he suggested.

But Old Trout only laughed, so that bubbles from the river bed rose and burst upon the surface.

"Courage," said he; "it will be an opportunity for you to learn the finer points of the game. If you are nervous, lie nearer to the bank. The natural fly does not drift there so abundantly, but you will be secure from the artificial. Presently I will treat you to an exhibition of playing with death you will not fail to appreciate." He broke off and pointed with his eyes. "Over you and to the left."

Rainbow made a neat double rise and drifted back into line. "Very mellow," he said—"very mellow and choice. Never tasted better. May I ask, sir, what you meant by piscine psychology?"

"I imply that my angler does not appreciate the subtle possibilities of our intellect. Now, my officer concerned himself as vitally with what we were thinking as with what we were feeding upon. This fellow, secure in the knowledge that his presentation is well-nigh perfect, is content to offer me the same variety of flies day after day, irrespective of the fact that I have learned them all by heart. I have, however, adopted the practice of rising every now and then to encourage him."

"Rising? At an artificial fly? I never heard such temerity in all my life," gasped Rainbow.

Old Trout moved his body luxuriously. "I should have said, appearing to rise," he amended. "You may have noticed that I have exhibited a predilection for small duns in preference to the larger *Ephemeridae*. My procedure is as follows: I wait until a natural dun and his artificial May fly are drifting downstream with the smallest possible distance separating them. Then I rise and take the dun. Assuming I have risen to him, he strikes, misses, and is at once greatly flattered and greatly provoked. By this device I sometimes occupy his attention for over an hour and thus render a substantial service to others of my kind who would certainly have fallen victim to his skill."

"The river is greatly in your debt, sir," said Young Rainbow, with deliberate satire.

He knew by experience that fish as well as anglers are notorious liars, but the exploit his host recounted was a trifle too strong. Taking a sidelong glance, he was surprised to see that Old Trout did not appear to have appreciated the subtle ridicule of his remark. The long, lithe body had become almost rigid and the great round eyes were focused upon the surface with an expression of fixed concentration.

Looking up, Rainbow saw a small white-winged May fly with red legs and a body the color of straw swing out from the main stream and describe a slow circle over the calm surface above Old Trout's head. Scarcely an inch away a tiny blue dun, its wings folded as closely as the pages of a book, floated attendant. An upward rush, a sucking kerr-rop, and when the broken water had calmed, the dun had disappeared and the May fly was dancing away downstream.

"Well," said Old Trout, "how's that, my youthful skeptic? Pretty work, eh?"

"I saw nothing in it," was the impertinent reply. "There is not a trout on the river who could not have done likewise."

"Even when one of those two flies was artificial?" Old Trout queried tolerantly.

"But neither of them was artificial," Rainbow retorted. "Had it been so, the angler would have struck. They always do."

"Of course he struck," Old Trout replied.

"But he didn't," Rainbow protested. "I saw the May fly go down with the current."

"My poor fish!" Old Trout replied. "Do you presume to suggest that I am unable to distinguish an artificial from a natural fly? Are you so blind that you failed to see the prismatic colors in the water from the paraffin in which the fly had been dipped? Here you are! Here it is again!"

Once more the white-winged insect drifted across the backwater, but this time there was no attendant dun.

"If that's a fake I'll eat my tail," said Rainbow.

"If you question my judgment," Old Trout answered, "you are at liberty to rise. I dare say, in spite of a shortage of brain, that you would eat comparatively well."

But Rainbow, in common with his kind, was not disposed to take chances.

"We may expect two or three more casts from this fly and then he will change it for a bigger. It is the same programme every day without a variation. How differently my officer would have acted. By now he would have discovered my little joke and turned the tables against me. Aye me, but some men will never learn! Your mental outfit, dear Rainbow, is singularly like a man's," he added. "It lacks elasticity."

Rainbow made no retort and was glad of his forbearance, for every word Old Trout had spoken was borne out by subsequent events. Four times the white-winged May fly described an arc over the backwater, but in the absence of duns Old Trout did not rise again. Then came a pause, during which, through a lull in the hatch, even the natural insect was absent from the river.

"He is changing his fly," said Old Trout, "but he will not float it until the hatch starts again. He is casting beautifully this morning and I hope circumstances will permit me to give him another rise."

"But suppose," said Rainbow breathlessly, "you played this game once too often and were foul hooked as a result?"

Old Trout expanded his gills broadly. "Why, then," he replied, "I should break him. Once round a limb of that submerged apple bough and the thing would be done. I should never allow myself to be caught and no angler could gather up the slack and haul me into midstream in time to prevent me reaching the bough. Stand by."

The shadow of a large, dark May fly floated cockily over

the backwater and had almost returned to the main stream when a small iron-blue dun settled like a puff of thistledown in its wake.

The two insects were a foot nearer the fast water than the spot where Old Trout was accustomed to take the rise. But for the presence of a spectator, it is doubtful whether he would have done so, but Young Rainbow's want of appreciation had excited his vanity, and with a rolling swoop he swallowed the dun and bore it downward.

And then an amazing thing happened. Instead of drifting back to his place as was expected, Old Trout's head was jerked sideways by an invisible force. A thin translucent thread upcut the water's surface and tightened irresistibly. A second later Old Trout was fighting, fighting, fighting to reach the submerged apple bough with the full weight of the running water and the full strength of the finest Japanese gut strained against him.

Watching, wide-eyed and aghast, from one of the underwater rat holes into which he had hastily withdrawn, Rainbow saw the figure of a man rise out of a bed of irises downstream and scramble upon the bank. In his right hand, with the wrist well back, he held a light split-cane rod whose upper joint was curved to a half-circle. The man's left hand was detaching a collapsible landing net from the ring of his belt. Every attitude and movement was expressive of perfectly organized activity. His mouth was shut as tightly as a steel trap, but a light of happy excitement danced in his eyes.

"No, you don't, my fellar," Rainbow heard him say. "No, you don't. I knew all about that apple bough before ever I put a fly over your pool. And the weed bed on the right," he added, as Old Trout made a sudden swerve half down and half across stream.

Tucking the net under his arm the man whipped up the slack with a lightning-like action. The maneuver cost Old Trout dear, for when, despairing of reaching the weed and burrowing into it, he tried to regain his old position, he found himself six feet farther away from the apple bough than when the battle began.

Instinctively Old Trout knew it was useless to dash downstream, for a man who could take up slack with the speed his adversary had shown would profit by the expedient to come more quickly to terms with him. Besides, lower down there was broken water to knock the breath out of his lungs. Even where he lay straining and slugging this way and that, the water was pouring so fast into his open mouth as nearly to drown him. His only chance of effecting a smash was by a series of jumps, followed by quick dives. Once before, although he had not confessed it to Rainbow, Old Trout had saved his life by resorting to this expedient. It takes the strain off the line and returns it so quickly that even the finest gut is apt to sunder.

Meanwhile the man was slowly approaching, winding up as he came. Old Trout, boring in the depths, could hear the click of the check reel with increasing distinctness. Looking up, he saw that the cast was almost vertical above his head, which meant that the moment to make the attempt was at hand. The tension was appalling, for ever since the fight began his adversary had given him the butt unremittingly. Aware of his own weight and power, Old Trout was amazed that any tackle could stand the strain.

"Now's my time," he thought, and jumped.

It was no ordinary jump, but an aerial rush three feet out of the water, with a twist at its apex and a cutting lash of the tail designed to break the cast. But his adversary was no ordinary angler, and at the first hint of what was happening he dropped the point of the rod flush with the surface.

Once and once more Old Trout flung himself into the air, but after each attempt he found himself with diminishing strength and with less line to play with.

"It looks to me," said Rainbow mournfully, "as if my unhappy host will lose this battle and finish up in that glass case to which he was referring a few minutes ago." And greatly affected, he burrowed his nose in the mud and wondered, in the event of this dismal prophecy coming true, whether he would be able to take possession of the pool without molestation.

In consequence of these reflections he failed to witness the last phase of the battle, when, as will sometimes happen with big fish, all the fight went out of Old Trout, and rolling wearily over and over, he abandoned himself to the clinging embraces of the net. He never saw the big man proudly carry Old Trout back into the hayfield, where, before proceeding to remove the fly, he sat down beside a shallow dike and lit a cigarette and smiled largely. Then, with an affectionate and professional touch, he picked up Old Trout by the back of the neck, his forefinger and thumb sunk firmly in the gills.

"You're a fine fellar," he said, extracting the fly; "a good sportsman and a funny fish. You fooled me properly for three days, but I think you'll own I outwitted you in the end."

Rummaging in his creel for a small rod of hard wood that he carried for the purpose of administering the quietus, he became aware of something that arrested his action. Leaning forward, he stared with open eyes at a tiny W perforated in the upper part of Old Trout's tail.

"Shades of the war! Dulverton!" he exclaimed. Then with a sudden warmth: "Old chap, old chap, is it really you? This is red-letter stuff. If you're not too far gone to take another lease of life, have it with me."

And with the tenderness of a woman, he slipped Old Trout into the dike and in a tremble of excitement hurried off to the *auberge* where the fisherman lodged, to tell a tale no one even pretended to believe.

For the best part of an hour Old Trout lay in the shallow waters of the dike before slowly cruising back to his own place beneath the overhanging bank. The alarming experience through which he had passed had made him a shade forgetful, and he was not prepared for the sight of Young Rainbow rising steadily at the hatch of fly.

"Pardon me, but a little more to your right," he said, with heavy courtesy.

"Diving otters!" cried Young Rainbow, leaping a foot clear of the water. "You, sir! You!"

"And why not?" Old Trout replied. "Your memory must be short if you have already forgotten that this is my place."

"Yes, but—" Rainbow began and stopped.

"You are referring to that little circus of a few minutes ago," said Old Trout. "Is it possible you failed to appreciate the significance of the affair? I knew at once it was my dear officer when he dropped the artificial dun behind the natural May fly. In the circumstances I could hardly do less than accept his invitation. Nothing is more delightful than a reunion of comrades of the war." He paused and added: "We had a charming talk, he and I, and I do not know which of us was the more affected. It is a tragedy that such friendship and such intellect as we share cannot exist in common element."

And so great was his emotion that Old Trout dived and buried his head in the weeds. Whereby Rainbow did uncommonly well during the midday hatch.

Mr. Theodore Castwell

G. E. M. Skues

Mr. Theodore Castwell, having devoted a long, strenuous and not unenjoyable life to hunting to their doom innumerable salmon, trout, and grayling in many quarters of the globe, and having gained much credit among his fellows for his many ingenious improvements in rods, flies, and tackle employed for that end, in the fullness of time died and was taken to his own place.

St. Peter looked up from a draft balance sheet at the entry of the attendant angel.

"A gentleman giving the name of Castwell. Says he is a fisherman, your Holiness, and has 'Fly-Fishers' Club, London' on his card."

"Hm-hm," says St. Peter. "Fetch me the ledger with his account."

St. Peter perused it.

"Hm-hm," said St. Peter. "Show him in."

Mr. Castwell entered cheerfully and offered a cordial right hand to St. Peter.

"As a brother of the angle—" he began.

"Hm-hm," said St. Peter. "I have been looking at your account from below."

"I am sure I shall not appeal to you in vain for special consideration in connection with the quarters to be assigned to me here."

"Hm-hm," said St. Peter.

"Well, I've seen worse accounts," said St. Peter. "What sort of quarters would you like?"

"Do you think you could manage something in the way of a country cottage of the Test Valley type, with modern conveniences and, say, three quarters of a mile of one of those pleasant chalk streams, clear as crystal, which proceed from out the throne, attached?"

"Why, yes," said St. Peter. "I think we can manage that for you. Then what about your gear? You must have left your fly rods and tackle down below. I see you prefer a light split cane of nine foot or so, with appropriate fittings. I will indent upon the Works Department for what you require, including a supply of flies. I think you will approve of our dresser's productions. Then you will want a keeper to attend you."

"Thanks awfully, your Holiness," said Mr. Castwell. "That will be first-rate. To tell you the truth, from the Revelations I read, I was inclined to fear that I might be just a teeny-weeny bit bored in heaven."

"In h-hm-hm," said St. Peter, checking himself.

It was not long before Mr. Castwell found himself alongside an enchantingly beautiful clear chalk stream, some fifteen yards wide, swarming with fine trout feeding greedily: and presently the attendant angel assigned to him had handed him the daintiest, most exquisite, light split-cane rod conceivable—perfectly balanced with the reel and line—with a beautifully damped tapered cast of incredible fineness and strength, and a box of flies of such marvelous tying as to be almost mistakable for the natural insects they were to simulate.

Mr. Castwell scooped up a natural fly from the water, matched it perfectly from the fly box, and knelt down to cast to a riser putting up just under a tussock ten yards or so above him. The fly lit like gossamer, six inches above the last ring; and next moment the rod was making the curve of beauty. Presently, after an exciting battle, the keeper netted out a beauty of about two and a half pounds.

"Heavens," cried Mr. Castwell. "This is something like."

"I am sure his Holiness will be pleased to hear it," said the keeper.

Mr. Castwell prepared to move upstream to the next riser when he noticed that another trout had taken up the position of that which he had just landed, and was rising. "Just look at that," he said, dropping instantaneously to his knee and drawing off some line. A moment later an accurate fly fell just above the neb of the fish, and instantly Mr. Castwell engaged in battle with another lusty fish. All went well, and presently the landing net received its two and a half pounds.

"A very pretty brace," said Mr. Castwell, preparing to move on to the next string of busy nebs which he had observed putting up around the bend. As he approached the tussock, however, he became aware that the place from which he had just extracted so satisfactory a brace was already occupied by another busy feeder.

"Well, I'm damned," said Mr. Castwell. "Do you see that?"

"Yes, sir," said the keeper.

The chance of extracting three successive trout from the same spot was too attractive to be forgone, and once more Mr. Castwell knelt down and delivered a perfect cast to the spot. Instantly it was accepted and battle was joined. All held, and presently a third gleaming trout joined his brethren in the creel.

Mr. Castwell turned joyfully to approach the next riser round the bend. Judge, however, his surprise to find that once more the pit beneath the tussock was occupied by a rising trout, apparently of much the same size as the others.

"Heavens," exclaimed Mr. Castwell. "Was there ever anything like it?"

"No, sir," said the keeper.

"Look here," said he to the keeper. "I think I really must give this chap a miss and pass on to the next."

"Sorry, it can't be done, sir. His Holiness would not like it."

"Well, if that's really so," said Mr. Castwell, and knelt rather reluctantly to his task.

Several hours later he was still casting to the same tussock.

"How long is this confounded rise going to last?" inquired Mr. Castwell. "I suppose it will stop soon."

"No, sir," said the keeper.

"What, isn't there a slack hour in the afternoon?"

"No afternoon, sir."

"What? Then what about the evening rise?"

"No evening rise, sir," said the keeper.

"Well, I shall knock off now. I must have had about thirty brace from that corner."

"Beg pardon, sir, but his Holiness would not like that."

"What?" said Mr. Castwell. "Mayn't I even stop at night?"

"No night here, sir," said the keeper.

"Then do you mean that I have got to go on catching these damned two-and-a-half pounders at this corner forever and ever?"

The keeper nodded.

"Hell!" said Mr. Castwell.

"Yes," said his keeper.

Retrospect

Viscount Grey of Fallodon

IN THE LATTER PART OF 1918 MY LAST BIT OF CENTRE VISION
was obscured and I descended at once on to a lower plane
of sight than I had yet experienced. Since then there has
been very slow deterioration, which is now perceptible even
as compared with 1918; but the great drop came when the
centre vision went: after that the difference between a little
more and a little less side vision is one of degree. It does not
add to the number of total disabilities that are imposed by the
loss of centre vision. By 1918 I had ceased to be able to see
a small fly floating on the water. It was, however, possible to
judge distance more accurately and to present a dry fly effec-
tively to a rising trout more frequently than I should have
supposed to be possible under such disadvantage. Nevertheless, it happened more than once in this season that I struck
to the sound of a rise without seeing it, and found that I had
hooked the trout for which I was trying. It had taken my fly
on the surface and I had failed to see the rise, even though my
eyes had been directed to the place where I knew the fish to
be. It was evident that for me the end of dry-fly fishing was

very near. It was so. When the season of 1919 came I could no longer see rises.

It would be possible still to get some trout on a dry fly with some one always in attendance to help me. The attendant would find a rising trout, would show me where to stand or to kneel: would describe the direction in and the distance to which the fly should be cast: would say when this had been done correctly: and finally would utter some exclamation when the fish took the fly, so that I might give the necessary strike. But the whole process would be intolerably cumbersome and clumsy, and I should bungle sadly. Skill in dry-fly fishing is denied to bad sight.

Nec vera virtus, cum semel exidit,
curat reponi deterioribus.

There remains wet-fly fishing for trout in still water and across or down stream. When there is no slack line, a certain proportion of trout—a good proportion when they are taking well—that come at an angler's fly will hook themselves. There is, of course, some bungling. With indistinct vision it is not easy to place the landing-net accurately under a trout, even when the fish is exhausted and can be held steady on the surface of the water, especially if this be a rippling stream. More than once recently, when wading in such water, where trout average four to the pound, has the mistake been made of placing the net carefully under a bit of foam, which, as the net was lifted, dissolved and disappeared like a mocking spirit. Nevertheless, the thing can be done still, independent and unaided, which is an essential part of the peculiar pleasure of trout fishing: and though my baskets are light there come bright gleams of success. The mere touch of a trout, even if it does not hook itself, gives a little thrill; the feel of a small, single-handed rod, its quick and delicate motion, and its response to the hand, are delightful: it is very pleasant to spend a day by rippling streams with a background of trees and the air lively with the songs of birds in April and May.

Salmon fishing is less difficult, though some of the pleasure is gone. It is twelve years since I have been able to see my fly fall on the water or to watch the line. These things were a matter of course in salmon fishing: not till I lost sight of them did I realize what an integral part of the interest of salmon fishing they were. The salmon angler watches the fall of his fly at each cast, and his eyes are ever on the draw of the stream on his line. To be deprived of the latter is an even greater loss than it is to be unable to see the fly fall on the water.

However good be the river or the beat on it, there must be many hours, and an occasional day, when the angler does not get a pull: and to fish hour after hour seeing only the rod and nothing of the line is a very blank business. On days of failure an angler may be said to go through four stages of feeling. He begins with Expectation: this is presently modified to Hope: after Hope has been long deferred the angler subsides into the stage of Resignation: finally as the day draws to a close he sinks into Despair. The angler who fishes without seeing his fly or line passes more quickly through the happier to the lower stages.

Every angler loses a certain proportion of the salmon that he hooks and plays. There are days of hard luck and of good luck in this matter, but taking figures over a period of days I used to estimate that my proportion of fish lost to fish landed was one in six. For example, in the ten good days on the Cassley, described in the preceding chapter, sixty salmon were hooked and fifty landed. Two of the ten salmon that escaped broke the line round rocks. As the hook had sufficiently firm hold to break a strong gut cast, it may be assumed that but for the exceptional misfortune of the rocks, these two fish would have been landed. Eight in sixty would thus have been the proportion of salmon lost owing to the hook coming out. This is not a proportion that should cause excessive annoyance, and I do not remember having suffered greatly from losing salmon before my sight was impaired. Since that time I have suffered very badly. In one black week on the Cassley a few years ago, out of twenty-two salmon hooked only seven were landed. None of those that escaped broke the line: the fly just came away unaccountably, often when the fish was almost within reach of the net.

In speaking of salmon "hooked" I include only the fish that have been actually played. Those that come to the surface immediately after being struck and splash themselves free are not counted; nor indeed are any salmon counted as "lost" if they have been held for quite a short time. In other words, only fish that have been not only hooked but played have been included in the calculation of fish lost. My experience that week was such as I hope no other angler may have to endure. A week that might have been happy and successful was turned to misery. My brother, who was fishing with me, hooked at least as many fish in those same six days, but did not lose an undue proportion and had a good week.

Things are, of course, not always so bad as in that week, or I should not be salmon fishing still. Nevertheless, the number of salmon hooked and played that I lose has been for the last twelve years very harassing. I cannot imagine why impaired sight should have caused this. It is not by sight, but by feel, that an angler strikes a salmon. In spring, salmon as a rule take the fly under water unseen: even if a fish does make a visible rise, the angler should not strike till the pull is felt. For this purpose it is an advantage not to see the rise. Why, then, should bad sight cause me to fail to hook fish securely? I can only suggest that the angler who watches the line coming round in the stream sees unconsciously, or half-consciously, the line tighten at the instant when he feels the pull of a fish: and that eyes and hands both being alert he strikes with more conviction than if he only felt and did not see. And to strike with conviction and not tentatively is necessary to hook salmon securely, especially with the big hooks that are used in spring.

Certainly since my sight was impaired I neither hook nor land as many fish as I used to do in comparison with others. The adverse change in this respect was very noticeable and persistent when my brother fished with me on the Cassley, where we could compare present with past experience on the same water. Some success still have, but the conclusion is irresistible that when a man ceases to be able to see what he is doing he does not do so well as he did before. The new method of salmon fishing with a greased line and comparatively small rod and fly presumably requires better sight than the ordinary method, and I have not tried it. It is by repute, and I dare say in practice, very effective, particularly in low water.

As long as there is a fair chance of getting fish the pleasure of fly fishing is to a very keen angler inexhaustible. It was, I think, Dr. Johnson who complained that he had never in his life had enough peaches. He therefore never knew, and we can never know, how many peaches would have satisfied him. In like manner, I shall never know for how many days I could fish continuously without wearying of it. Trout fishing has always been intermittent: of spring salmon fishing I have had, as a rule, from ten to twenty days in the season, and not more than ten days at a time. Would a keen golfer be satisfied if he played golf on from ten to twenty days only in the year? I suspect he would not, and I am sure that this allowance of salmon fishing is not satisfying. On the occasions when I have had a continuous spell of salmon fishing, I have quitted the river with as much regret at the end of the fifth or sixth week as I should have felt at the end of the first.

On the other hand, one does become more fastidious as to the kind of sport. To catch fresh run salmon spoils the interest in red or dark fish. The latter may give good sport, but to land a tarnished fish when an angler has been used to the brilliant

excellence of fresh run spring salmon, gives a sense of dissatis-
faction that blunts the edge of keenness.

Most men have to earn their own living and have little
enough opportunity for indulging in pleasure, even if they
have keenness. But any really keen angler who has not had to
work from necessity, and yet has not spent the whole of each
season in fly fishing, may say, as Clive said when he reflected
on his opportunities of acquiring wealth in India, that he is
astonished at his own moderation.

The moderation imposed on any one who undertakes
important work in life may be very distressing. I recall, in particular, a certain bitter moment in the latter half of April, 1909.
In 1906 and 1907 I had had no spring salmon fishing at all.
In 1908 I had ten days, but the Cassley was low: I got only
two salmon: in the whole time there was hardly any water in
which to throw a fly. My days were spent walking about the
moors in the April sunshine. "Not a bad way of spending a
holiday," some one may say. True, but it was not the thing for
which I had paid rent or which I had come to do, and it was
not satisfying to a man who had not caught a spring salmon
for three years.

In 1909 I came to the Cassley again and this time the
river was in order. After three years of abstinence or failure,
the prospect of good fishing was before me. On the first day
I had five fish by four o'clock; this was equal to the best day
I had ever had up to that time. The little post-office where I
was staying was only a hundred yards from the river. I came

in to see what the Foreign Office had sent me. There was an alarmist telegram about the state of things in Constantinople. I decided that I must return to London. It was then too late to get the evening train: I went back to the river and got one more salmon, making what was then a record for me. The next morning I left: the river was still in order; there was the prospect of a week of good sport if only I could stay: there was the certainty that I must wait a whole year before I could spring-salmon fish again. And there was not even the compensation of feeling a martyr to duty. If the disturbances at Constantinople became dangerous, British action must be limited to protecting British lives and property. The measures necessary for this would be taken by the diplomatic and naval authorities on the spot, whether I were at the Foreign Office or not. If I stayed at the Cassley till something really happened I could be at the Foreign Office in plenty of time to deal with political complications that might arise later on, the public interest would not suffer if I awaited developments. But the fear of what would be said in the House of Commons and in the Press, if something did happen and I were absent from my office, destroyed my equanimity: I went back to London feeling cowardly rather than noble, and not at all convinced that the sacrifice made was necessary. The event proved that it was unnecessary.

Such misfortune and disappointment leave a mark on memory, but it is an isolated incident. When the angler looks back he sees a long vista of happy days: by a special act of

memory he can select individual days of outstanding success, but even these seem not to be exceptions; they are but
contributory parts of an enjoyment that was greater than any
single day could contain. For to an angler as he looks back, his
angling days seem to belong to a world different from, and
fairer than, the world in which he has worked. In retrospect
the surroundings, the country, the beauty of river scenes are an
inseparable part of the pleasure. The keen angler may indeed
be comparatively indifferent to them when actively engaged in
fishing. If a rare and beautiful bird had appeared in a Hampshire water-meadow when trout were rising and I was busy
with them, what would the effect on my fishing have been?
My impression is that I should have made a mental note of it,
resolved to look for and watch the bird when the rise of trout
was over, and have continued to fish without interruption. So
intense is the interest and excitement of fly fishing when we
are actively engaged in it. On the other hand, if I could again
fish with a dry fly I should not now take a fishing, unless it
was in beautiful country. The fact that the water meadows
where I fished on the Itchen were one of the fairest spots in
the world became an ever-increasing part in the enjoyment.
This enhanced the anticipation of going thither; it made the
days spent there radiant.

The cottage that I put up by the Itchen in 1890 was
intended only as a fishing cottage; a place in which to get
food, sleep, and shelter when I was not fishing. It became a
sanctuary. The peace and beauty of the spot made it a sacred

place. The cottage belongs to angling memories, but the fishing became a small part of the happiness that was associated with it. For thirty-three years the chosen spot remained a place of refuge and delight, not in the fishing season only. For the last four years, indeed, I had been unable to fish with a dry fly, and the original purpose for which the cottage had been put there had ceased to be. Great changes, however, had been taking place that were inseparable from a new epoch. For the first fifteen years there was little change and had been little change for many years before that time. I had seen the old mill at the village not far away replaced by a new building, and the dull, monotonous sound of a turbine had replaced the lively splashing of a waterwheel; but otherwise things remained as they were. The cottage was invisible from any road; it was approached by an old lime avenue, long disused, and the track down this was not suited for any wheels but those of a farm cart. There was a little wayside station on a single railway line close by; but the quickest route from London was to go by a fast train to Winchester, and thence to drive a distance between four and five miles to the nearest point to the cottage that was accessible by wheels. This was a drive of at least half an hour in a one-horse fly. Presently taxicabs took the place of the horse conveyance and reduced the time of the drive to a quarter of an hour. Was this an advantage? On balance, it was not. For escape from London meant that hurry, noise and bustle had been left behind: I had entered into leisure, where saving of time was no object, and often I would walk from

Winchester to enjoy the country. There was a footpath way on each side of the river. By one of these one entered the cottage without, except for the momentary crossing of one road and of three secluded lanes, having had touch or sight of a road. There were thirty-three stiles on this path. It happened not infrequently that I could not get to Winchester till the latest train arriving there some time after eleven o'clock. The walk then lasted well into the midnight hour. In the dusk or dark it was easier to walk by the road than by the path. There was much charm in this midnight walk. Traffic had ceased, cottage lights had been put out, the inmates were all at rest or asleep. Now and then one heard, in passing, the song of a nightingale or a sedge-warbler, but in the main there was silence. It was pleasant after the hardness of London streets and pavements to feel the soft dust about my feet. On a still summer night there were sweet and delicate scents in the air, breathed forth from leaves and herbs and grass, and from the earth itself. It was as if one's own very being was soothed and in some way refined by the stillness, the gentleness and the sweetness of it all.

Then came the age of motors and tarred roads. Few people, I imagine, seek the smell of tar for its own sake. To me there is nothing unclean or nauseous in it, but it is a coarse, rough smell. The sweet and delicate scents of the night were obliterated by it, as if, overpowered and repelled, they had sunk back into the leaves and earth from which they had ventured into air. The strong smell of the tar seemed to disturb even the stillness of the night; the soft dust was no more, and the road was hard as a paved street. Not all, but much of the charm of the night walk was gone. There were other changes too; small houses of the villa type were built along the road that was nearest to the cottage: doubtless there are more of them now, for the cottage was accidentally destroyed by fire in January, 1923, and I have not seen the place for some years. The sense of change was in the air. It may be that change is for the good:

> *The old order changeth, yielding place to new,*
> *And God fulfils himself in many ways,*
> *Lest one good custom should corrupt the world.*

It is not for us, who cannot forsee the future, who perhaps cannot rightly understand the present, to chide or to repine too much. Only it is impossible for us, who in our youth gave our affections to things that are passed or passing away, to transfer our affections to new things in which a new generation finds delight.

The beauty, however, of chalk-strewn valleys still remains wonderful. The river still waters meadows that are unspoilt and unchanged, and its clear purity is guarded and protected.

> *Still glides the stream and shall for ever glide,*
> *The form remains, the function never dies.*

Thus, as the angler looks back he thinks less of individual captures and days than of the scenes in which he fished. The luxuriance of water meadows, animated by insect and bird and trout life, tender with the green and gay with the blossoms of early spring: the nobleness and volume of great salmon rivers: the exhilaration of looking at any salmon pool, great or

small; the rich brownness of Highland water: the wild open-
ness of the treeless, trackless spaces which he has traversed in
an explorer's spirit of adventure to search likely water for sea
trout: now on one, now on another of these scenes an angler's
mind will dwell, as he thinks of fishing. Special days and suc-
cesses he will no doubt recall, but always with the remem-
brance and the mind's vision of the scenes and the world in
which he fished. For, indeed, this does seem a separate world,
a world of beauty and enjoyment. The time must come to all
of us, who live long, when memory is more than prospect. An
angler who has reached this stage and reviews the pleasure of
life will be grateful and glad that he has been an angler, for he
will look back upon days radiant with happiness, peaks and
peaks of enjoyment that are not less bright because they are lit
in memory by the light of a setting sun.